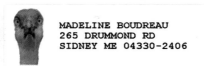

The Franciscan Charism

in the Third Millennium

by

Anselm W. Romb, OFM CONV.

ISBN # 0-913382-64-7

Printed and bound in the U. S. A. by
McNaughton & Gunn, Inc.
960 Woodland Drive
Saline Michigan 48176

 Published by the Marytown Press
1600 W. Park Avenue
Libertyville IL 60048

Dedication

to the
Franciscan Sisters of Chicago (Lemont)
for whom this book was originally conceived
twenty-five years ago;

and to my dear confreres, OFM CONV.,
Fr. Philip Wozniak
Fr.. Luke Poczworowski
Fr. Anthony Labedis
Fr. Aloysius Romanowski
my fellow travelers on the Franciscan journey;

and to the Franciscan Brothers of the Annunciation
Gabriel Ward
Raphael Guzzo
Anthony Burns
for their close friendship
and brotherly concern over many hurdles
many trials
many years

fondly
prayerfully
lovingly

by the author

Acknowledgments

My profound thanks to Judy Kozak for typing the manuscript so professionally from my potpourri of notes, hand written intercalations and the text from twenty-five years ago.

To Peter Ptak SFO, my friend and the focus and foundation of the Marytown Press in Libertyville, Illinois go my admiration and thanks for his computer craftsmanship and design for this book.

There are always "angels" who help to bring a book to completion. The angels who funded this book are Tom and Colleen Rossitto of Omaha.

–Fr. Anselm W. Romb. OFM CONV.

Table of Contents

Foreword

The original contents of this book were published under the title of *The Franciscan Charism in the Church* in 1969. Since then religious life, including the Franciscan Order, has developed and changed, for better or for worse, depending on one's vantage point. Meanwhile, following the demise of the St. Anthony Guild Publishing Company of Paterson, New Jersey, there have been many calls to republish *Franciscan Charism*. Nevertheless, in the light of the past quarter century, it might be helpful to re-examine the postulates and axioms of this book. After twenty-five years this volume has doubled in size and (one hopes) insights.

I continue to alternate in my roles of Diogenes, looking for an honest Franciscan, and Savanarola, despairing whether I ever found one. In any case this book must finally be judged as it is presented, namely, as one man's opinion.

Introduction: Response and Repetition

Of himself man is unable to explain the riddles of the universe. This does not refer to the phenomena which impinge upon him as a sensory-perceptual organism. On the contrary, despite his growing scientific knowledge, man retains his anxiety about a possible framework within which such phenomena occur. Orderliness, interpersonal relationships, sanction, immortality, priority of values—each person individually imposes a framework according to his struggles and his lights.

This framework can and has been derived by some men without reference to a transcendent being. Others are led— or often driven—by a variety of arguments to affirm the existence of a Creator as the source and ground of their framework. But every such affirmation becomes a unique statement by each person who makes it. The *assent* of the mind to a divine principle of one's being never occurs without a simultaneous *consent* of the will. More accurately, the *whole person* chooses to understand the universe in the special light of faith, generally with an emotional dimension of exhilaration, or relief, or even foreboding. In this sense faith is not communicable between men; it can barely even be described. The Creator must intervene and enter one's personal salvation history.

The broadest notion of faith is a trusting response to another person's superior experience. The believer, persuaded by another's credentials, replaces his inexperience with knowledge that can be observed and verified in another's actions. With respect to religious faith, a person is constrained to search out another with superior experience or comes upon one who claims to possess it.

Even the persons who have been indoctrinated in a particular religious faith from childhood must seek out or be converted by the testimony of another's superior experience of God. As adults they must give assent and consent to the doctrines and values of their creed. By its nature faith includes a certain submission. Mohammed made this concept central to belief in his message; *Islam* means "submission." The immediate consequence of faith is a relative security and awareness of purpose in the universe, based on God's entry into in human history through those men and women who are open to the divine communications.

But the sense of security and purpose is merely a placebo, a rationalization, and a cowardly escape from human striving, unless a fundamental motive force, stemming from man's own nature, is concomitant with faith. This motive force is not supernatural in itself, nor is it a cause of faith. It is, rather, a *catalyst*, typically present with *mature* faith. This catalyst appears to be threefold: man's awareness of his own perfectibility, his aspiration to encompass all the world in his mind, and his drive to experience whatever is possible to the human state. Of course, inasmuch as God uses many means to sanctify man, a theologian would see these natural qualities as "actual graces" to the degree that they developed under divine inspiration.

Further, it is the balanced and flexible personality with a goodly tolerance of ambivalence which can take the risk of faith and remain poised at the juncture of the city of God and the city of man. Or rather, the man of faith consciously attempts to make the two cities coextensive with each other. For him, the perfectibility of man and his desire to experience whatever exists is never accomplished without an investigation of others' claims to knowledge of the transcendent God and his immanent manifestions.

God reveals himself in many ways according to the condition and conditioning of men in their evolutionary struggle. Each self-revelation of God, if it is a genuine one, remains forever valid. Although God is simple and uncluttered by nature, man both as an individual and as a member of a social group understands God differently-through an accumulation of insights and relationships. Thus the God of the Old Testament gave the supreme commandment to love him and one's neighbor quite explicitly. Nevertheless the Israelites understood the mode of loving God and the identity of one's neighbor rather narrowly, until the prophets and subsequent leaders expanded the meaning of these relationships.

For Christians the fullness of God's self-revelation is the Word-made-flesh, Jesus Christ. He claimed the unique experience of being totally human and absolutely divine. As a prophet he also revealed this slowly and cumulatively, allowing his listeners then and now to absorb the communication by degrees. The person who searches for God during his adult years, if he intends to share in the Christian experience, must sooner or later be evangelized. That is, he must listen to the claims of Christ and submit himself, realizing that he is ignorant of the full relationship he might have with God.

Christ, moreover, shows himself as the son of God in the denotative sense of having the same nature. In the religions which existed prior to Christ, sonship was not an uncommon concept, but the term was merely connotative. Nevertheless, the connotations of providential care and individual interest were also very precise dimensions of Christ's teaching about the divine paternity. Yet no one, Christ asserted, comes to the Father (in this full sense) unless the Son reveals him. In the third strophe of the Prologue to St. John's Gospel, the writer tells us, "Any who did accept him he empowered to become children of God. These are they who believe in his name" (verse 12). In the fifth strophe the author proclaims Christ's unique and superior experience: "No one has ever seen God. It is God, the only Son, ever at his Father's side, who has revealed him" (verse 18).

To sum up, we can say that the Christian believer *responds* submissively—not cravenly—to Christ's claim to know the heavenly Father from the experience of his own sonship. The community of those who believe in him, that is, the Church of Christ, is the continuation of his mission to the world. The believer with mature faith and therefore integral personality attempts to enter into and *repeat* the experience of Christ as the Son of God. According to their natural talents and supernatural gifts the members of the Christian community struggle to extend the personality and mission of Christ among men. Such is the context into which we must place all activities of Christian believers. This, of course, includes religious life in all of its forms. *Response* and *repetition* are the key words of faith in God through Jesus Christ; they are implicit in the vocabulary of Francis of Assisi.

Francis responded to Jesus' claim that he was God's Son and uniquely able to lead us to his Father. Francis repeated Jesus' lifestyle, yet he did not "discover" the Gospel, because it was present in Europe for eleven centuries. But the Gospel was dormant. It would be hypercritical and insensitive to the great monastic Orders to declare that they did not know nor practice the Gospel in the centuries prior to Francis of Assisi, because their perception of the Gospel produced saints and scholars aplenty.

It was Francis' task to "re-invent" the Gospel life even in its externals. Just as the thirteenth was not the first century, so the twenty-first century is neither. So every century has to re-invent Franciscan life and, in a sense, re-interpret Francis himself.

A common anxiety of the young and not-so-young is his or her worthiness and competence to re-invent Gospel life. Who is holy, prayerful and zealous enough? Who is prepared with the natural dimensions of talent and strength? In the first chapter of Jeremiah the prophet resisted his vocation, claiming that he was too young to speak. But the Lord answered that Jeremiah should go wherever he was to be sent and without fear because the Lord's words were in his mouth. So Francis vacillated in his vocation until the Lord's words were fully his. In II Corinthians, chapter 5, St. Paul encourages us, "If anyone is in Christ, he is a new creation. The old order has passed away; now all is new."

To be filled with God's words, we must be emptied of our own—our own desires, needs, ambitions. This is a timeless truth. When we re-invent Franciscan life in the 21st century, self-emptiness remains a requirement. To *respond* to Jesus' claim and *repeat* his words are the keys to faithful action always, but the upcoming century will have its own specifications. Priest, religious, and layperson must respond to and repeat the Lord's words for the third millenium of Christianity (that is, if there is to be one!). Do you recall the great relief when the first millenium passed without the end-time?

What if the scenario of the third millenium goes something like this? The euphoria of a third millenium beginning will breed a new optimism in the industrialized nations after safely passing the year 2000, which was supposed to be for many a terrifying turning point. In the "have-not" nations there will arise a more powerful demand for a share in the world's resources and technologies that will lead to hostilities and power struggles. Africa, whose population will be decimated by AIDS, warfare, and tribalism, will be a magnet for migrations from Asia. Europe will be on its guard from that old canard, *pan-Slavism*. The Americas will gradually combine into their own economic empire, but the U.S. must learn to surrender its persistent hegemony. World religions will re-inforce their doctrines and draw up battle lines that will re-verse the small gains of ecumenism. There will be less exploi-tation of the poor and of the poor nations, but they will have to set a warlike agenda to escape being *controlled*. After a few years the social and moral values will make a half-hearted return to stricter control, but that future is uncertain, due to the high incidence of crime. Nuclear winters and summer global warming, epidemics and famine, the population ex-plosion, increased pollution---all these become moral issues that will and must be addressed by the Franciscan presence. In any case, the paragraph above is only one man's prophecy!

Is it any wonder that the Gospel will have to be re-dis-covered, Jesus re-interpreted, and Franciscanism re-defined in the third millenium? As technology has increased, rather than solved our problems; as sociology, psychology, and the behavioral sciences have lost their impact and influence; as politics and economics have become increasingly "dirty"; what else can we do than bring faith-action into play? First, the world must be emptied out of its pseudo-solutions to leave room for divine solutions. The world has its own philosophy (remarkably effective in creating and achieving goals) and will continue to resist the Gospel to the end. To paraphrase the master, Soren Kierkegaard, when the world and the Gospel reconcile, it is either the end of the Gospel as we know it, or the end of the world!

Jesus himself taught us the message of dying to oneself to overcome the world. In Philippians 2:6-11, we read that the Lord, when among us in the flesh, did not cling to his divine status, but took our vulnerable nature into the realm of death itself. As a result, his Father accorded him a name above all others so that the whole universe would proclaim that Jesus is the Lord God. Nor can we share in the words of Christ until we are mute; we will not gain the victory of praising Jesus until we have learned silence about ourselves.

In order to replicate the mind and activities of Jesus, Francis had to subordinate his gifts, personality, and liberty itself to become free. Francis had to surrender the "delicious" feelings of self-pity and self-deprecation of his early stages of conversion and accept his worth and value that came from Jesus having loved him first. Francis had to accept the overwhelming and compelling love from God so that it overflowed into a general and universal love for all men and women. For Francis it was the vowed life that made these self-renunciations effective: to "live the Gospel of our Lord Jesus Christ by living in obedience, without anything of (his) own, and in chastity." (The Second Rule of 1223) Always it had to happen for the Kingdom of God, otherwise, living poorly was just another kind of misery, living celibately might be a special brand of selfishness, living obediently would end up the lack of ambition and adequate motivation, not wanting to struggle with the world.

Faith in Jesus Christ and responding to and repeating his claims implies the whole Paschal Mystery. Dying to self means little without resurrection and becoming a new creation (II Corinthians 5:16). The gift (or charism) of Francis of Assisi to the world and to the Church is the theme of this book. In a sense, Franciscans start all over again in every century, in every nation to re-apply, re-interpret, re-invent the Gospel. They follow the Founder in turning their gaze backward to Christ in order to move forward to the Kingdom and the Second Coming of Jesus. From the faith of one man, Francis, grew the faith-community, the fraternity, which keeps re-inventing the Franciscan Order, not just the religious, but the Secular Franciscans, too. They repair the Church which is always in danger of "falling into ruins." Franciscans keep asking, as did Francis at each passing birthday, "When will we begin to serve the Lord?" The answer must not be the cliches of journeys and ephemeral dreams and sighing on a mountaintop and poetic fantasies, but realistic, down-to-earth practical answers.

The words of the Founder suggest the requirement of many, even daily conversions, laying up treasures in heaven where they remain secure. It is not that his faith left him hanging from heaven and out of touch with earth. It is precisely the opposite; Francis knew that earth is not necessarily evil, but terribly seductive; it demanded that he prove himself by being productive, taking command, and acquiring the works of success. He had to resist the expectations of his family, the lust of the eyes, and the pride of life.

Each conversion meant a deepening of faith, a renewal, leaving something behind and assuming something new. In sickness he had to stop worrying about his health; he turned away from being a playboy and grew serious and reflective. In kissing a leper he surrendered his sensitivity and assumed the marginal status of the sick and poor and rejected. In rebuilding the chapel of San Damiano he gave up the arrogance of wealth and class and accepted the status of a beggar and lowly stonemason.

With each conversion and increase of faith Francis realized his motives for entering God's service were mixed, perhaps sometimes self-indulgent (who can be so sure?). By the time he had fully turned around his inner and outer life, he knew that from the beginning it was not important throughout his innumerable faith-conversions why he came, but only why he stayed!

The emptying process, learning to repeat the words of Christ, and acting out of love is summarized in Colossians 3:2-17, "Be intent on things above rather than on things of earth. After all, you have died!.... Put to death whatever in your nature is rooted in earth.... Put on a new man, one who grows in knowledge as he is formed anew in the image of his Creator.... Let the word of Christ, rich as it is, dwell in you."

The several early "careers" of Francis indicated that he resisted sudden, complete, and irrevocable conversion, and that God remonstrated with him by the concomitant failures of the young man. It was "the carrot and the stick" from the start, and love and dread as the responses. Jesus asked his disciples, "Will you go up to Jerusalem to die with me?"

Whereas the habit, tau cross, or Franciscan cord do confer today identify, mission, and status, the patched robe and rope of Francis conferred nothing but ignominy and scorn in his day. He had to earn his Gospel identity, give evidence of his mission, and be affirmed in his status by the beneficiaries of his ministry, especially the poor. And here I touch upon the nature of charism itself, the secondary theme of this book. "Charism" is also a response of faith; it is the repetition of the life of Jesus in oneself and others.

In the Bible, that continually expanding self-revelation of God, we see a double phenomenon evolve in the community of God. This phenomenon is the mode by which God involves himself in the lives of those who are accessible to his communications. The mode creates a polarity, rather than a dichotomy within the mission of the Temple and of the Church.

CHAPTER I

Charism Evolves from Baptism

On the one hand, there developed a very formal and ritualistic structure to be the ordinary liaison between God and man. This was the levitical priesthood serving the altar of the Temple, coupled—at a later date—with the worship of the local congregation in the synagogue. In the theocratic framework of Israel the religious leaders were often political leaders and judges as well.

On the other hand, we read of the non-hierarchical expressions of the religious community. Such were the schools of prophetism, sometimes under the guidance of a well-known mouthpiece of God, who was a kind of *guru* to his followers. Discovery of the Qumran Scrolls, moreover, bears witness to the existence of groups similar to Christian religious orders in many respects, but also like the mystery cults popular in the Near East. Groups like the Essenes proposed to live a life that intensified the ordinary commitment to Israel's covenant with God. In addition to these currents within Judaism that thrived independently of, yet not divorced from the Temple, there were the nazirites. Samson and John the Baptist come to mind; they were dedicated to the ascetical and at times to the eremitical life. They hearkened back to the Israelites in Exodus, wandering as the Spirit dictated, dependent upon the largesse of nature, and rather isolated in purification from the earthbound people surrounding them. The prophets, whether so ascetical or not, more directly involved themselves in the spiritual life of the total community, serving as points of contact with God apart from the hierarchy. Their "schools" were probably the training ground for popular preachers and mystical theologians. Such schools were in contrast to the rabbinical schools, like that of Gamaliel, under whom St. Paul studied. The latter groups were oriented to official religion, the canons of Judaism, and the dogmatic interpretation of the Scriptures and prescriptions of behavior for the believer.

The history of the Old Testament reveals the manifold religious life within the ancient covenant. As Christians re-cite in the Creed, they express their belief in "the Holy Spirit, the Lord and Giver of life, who spoke through the prophets." The structures of Judaism were constantly being renewed or "updated" by the inspiration of the Spirit of God, breathing where it chose. This self-revelation of God to individual proph-ets, nazirites, and founders of religious groups is the personal *charism* or insight that individual possessed—or rather, which possessed him. This charism was the source of the individual's *enthusiasm*, a word which means "God within" or "within God."

It would be a grave error to make too sharp a division or separation between the hierarchy of Israel and charismatic persons, as though these were completely separate entities. The proper concept is rather one of polarization, whereby the interests and values of one group often are in tension with those of the other. But we must remain aware that any member of either group, that is, any member of God's community, could and can receive a charism. Historically, many of the formal rituals and behavioral prescriptions developed by charismatic persons were adopted by the hierarchy and even imposed in a crystallized form upon the universal membership. (A case in point is auricular confession of sins, introduced by Christian monks in the early Middle Ages among those whom they evangelized.) Members of the hierarchy of Israel, in order to be effective, would also have been the vehicles of a personal charism, if they were alert to it. This was their "grace of office."

The analogies between religious expression in the Temple and in the Church are readily apparent. The Spirit of God addresses himself to every accessible person. In the new covenant that same Spirit quickens the Body of Christ. St. Paul analyzed the multiple charisms in his local foundations. Individuals were given gifts to preach, to nurse, to educate, to speak in and interpret glossolalia. The spiritual gift was joined to the natural talent of an individual. Most important was the use of the gift for the benefit of and with the approval of the community. As in Israel, the charism need not put its possessors in opposition to the hierarchy, for charism belongs to the hierarchy as well as to others; bishops and theologians, for example, have their own charisms. We might say that the supreme charism of truth resides in the Bishop of Rome to the degree that he is accessible to the operations of the Spirit.

The centuries of the Church's existence have given rise to many specialized individual and group experiences parallel to those of Israel. Whether these experiences were uniquely personal or pertained to an entire religious movement, they were intensifications of the covenant of sonship proposed in the Gospel. Religious founders made their *response* of faith go beyond what Christians typically vow in baptism. Although every Christian is obliged to seek perfection through the evangelical counsels of poverty, chastity, and obedience, founders of religious orders and their adherents propose to *intensify* their baptismal vow. They usually make a public commitment, acceptable to the Church, to *repeat* the life of Christ in a pattern suited to the temper and needs of their times. This is their charism. It is a gift that stands in peril of extinction once it has become linked to an institutional framework. So we have seen religious institutes fall into desuetude. But, once again it must be emphasized, the polarities of "objectivized" communication from God through ordinary, even bureaucratic channels and the "subjectivized" inspiration received extraordinarily by individuals should not be understood too rigidly. Every charism must be consonant with the mission of the Church. On the other hand, without the innovative direction supplied by charismatic persons to the body politic, the Church would remain static, inflexible, condemned to rigidity.

All Christians, as we said, are bound to perfection. This commitment is convalidated by pronouncing one's baptismal vow—or at least by the mature recognition of the implications of baptism as an adult. In this sense even "born Catholics" need evangelization, which ideally should occur before the sacrament of Confirmation. (Perhaps some of the religious and priests who gravitated into their state of life without such an adult commitment to Christ are among those who are leaving their ministry in the time of crisis.)

To "come to perfection as your heavenly Father is perfect" (Matt. 5:48), as the New Testament states, has the meaning of being "complete" or "integral" as a person by becoming a son or daughter of God. Grace, which is a share in the Trinitarian life of God, uniquely provides this experience. Thus the man of faith repeats the life of reincarnated Christ upon earth. This repetition is contingent upon the life style which one chooses or to which one is conditioned by his personal history. The Christian struggle lies in making Christ present to the community, and to the world at large according to one's own perceptions.

The different expressions of religious life in the various Orders, as well as outside the framework of an institute, are all individual charisms that bespeak the continuing response of faith. Each expression needs the approval of the believing community to ensure its value. Typically the hierarchy voices its approval as the spokesman for the community. Nevertheless, many new charisms in the Church had to struggle for years and prove their relevance before they were recognized as coming from the Spirit. Even when members of the hierarchy were insensitive, however, the work of God could not be stopped, as long as the possessors of the charism were attuned to the divine communication. Whereas "official" or institutional approval may have been tardy, the validity of the charism was implemented by the non-official community, which was being built up by the charism. If the official leaders were uncomfortable, it was because they have the serious obligation to preserve and balance the enduring aspects of Church life. The very notion of "balance" connotes a precarious condition. Although St. Vincent de Paul and St. Francis de Sales, for example, tried to keep their concept of unstructured religious life viable, their foundations were nevertheless trapped into existing frameworks. When St. Francis of Assisi proposed his mobile and uncluttered rule of Gospel life to the Pope, the latter was unwilling to approve until a Cardinal pointed out that refusing approval was tantamount to denying that the life of Christ could be relived.

Despite the paragraph above, one cannot avoid the canonical ideal of a vocation as being a "call" from lawful Church superiors who stand in the place of God when they accept individuals into a new status within the Body of Christ. Ultimately this approval is what differentiates the religious from the typical Christian. Certainly anyone or any group can propose to live the Gospel life in an intensified way. But the religious are to *exhibit an official example of how a community of Christians—or just one Christian—makes Christ present to the world.* This modality of official approval historically has become an essential note of religious life as a charism within God's people. As we read in Section 45 of *Lumen Gentium*, the document of the Second Vatican Council on the mystery of the Church, religious life is essentially the public profession of the evangelical counsels.

Although religious life, as it is presently lived, *typically* includes the taking of vows and living the common life, its foundation is the *public profession* of the counsels. Therefore, isolates (such as exclaustrated religious) and so-called "lay" religious, who do not live the common life, are true religious even in the canonical sense. The term "public" means that the Church officially recognizes the individual or group to be professors of the Gospel life. Thus a person who promises before a bishop or his delegate to live the evangelical counsels is officially a religious, even if the promise were to have been made in secret, as has happened so often in recent years within the former communist enclaves. The consequence is that the official Church assumes the obligation to provide spiritual direction for that person's spiritual growth and engagement in the divinely ordained mission of the Church. Conversely, a person who stands before a thousand others and promises to live the Gospel life, but without official recognition of this charism, is still professing the counsels privately. Naturally, it goes without saying, private profession may be most perfect, pleasing to God, and with sacramentality for the believing community. The person who makes such a promise may be considered a "free-lance" religious without a title to the Church's direction any more special than the Christian who made no such profession.

Because the profession of the counsels may be made and lived even without oath-taking, vows as such do not appear to be an essential of the religious state. Thus Franciscan "secular" tertiaries can share in the charism of religious life without pronouncing vows. Nor do we have any record that all the early virgins, hermits, or ascetics bound themselves by vows. It is apparent that many of them, if not most, lived no common life. The virgins generally stayed with their families. Yet the Church gave recognition to their lives by assigning them a special place during the community worship. Theirs was a modality of the Gospel life that received the approval of the hierarchy.

Chapter Six of *Lumen Gentium* points out that the Church regulates and establishes enduring forms for interpreting poverty, chastity, and obedience (Section 43). The religious state is not a midpoint between the clergy and laity, but rather draws its members from both groups (Section 43). Religious divorce themselves from obstacles that hinder the fervor of charity and divine worship, so that they can devote themselves to the welfare of the entire Church (Section 44). They thereby become a sign that attracts others to fulfill their Christian vocations; they become an eschatological sign of the Church in the glory of perfected love (Section 44). As has been said above, religious life as a charism is outside the hierarchy, yet brings it new life (Section 44). The religious institute's particular insight into the Gospel is the source of its special energy or enthusiastic joy.

Because single or group religious life represents an intensification of the baptismal vow, it does not belong to its members alone. The whole Church, after official recognition, becomes aware of the charism and is concerned about that form of the Christ-life. (Analogously, the whole Church is interested in celibacy as an adjunct to the priesthood, because the priesthood of Christ, according to St. Peter's Epistle, is shared in by all the baptized.) Nevertheless, even though the metamorphosis of an institute's external works, prayer life, and customs falls under the jurisdiction of the hierarchy, only the possessors of the charism can appraise the validity of the changes. For this reason the recent Vatican Council alerted religious foundations to recover the spirit of their founders. But what of those institutes which decide that their lives need a complete overhauling, in order to keep their charism viable, and yet to whom the hierarchy does not grant leave? They must first of all be obedient to God, remove themselves from officialdom, and courageously "reduce" themselves from an approved institute, and search for their identity as a "free-lance" group. Perhaps at some future date they may seek the seal of approval again. It is a sad thought, however, that the institutional Church is not large enough to garner into its framework all the life styles of religious life, because charism is a "many-splendored thing."

Members who are indifferent to updating their special spirit are actually betraying their institute. Traditions should be reverenced without being irrevocably canonized. The spirit of the charism gives life, but external forms can become op-pressive. Now religious institutes—including their "lay" af-filiates, as Third Order fraternities—are urged to trace their spiritual ancestry back to Christ, but through their founders, who were communicated a special gift of understanding the Christ-life.

Any life style chosen by a Christian can be the best way for him to respond to and repeat the life of Christ begun in baptism. In their particular pattern, religious seem to have caught the parallels between baptismal and religious profes-sion. The local community scrutinizes its potential members and subjects them to a catechumenate before initiation. Wit-nesses for the community attest to the candidates' worthiness and sponsor the new members as they pronounce their credo. The latter are given a badge or garment to token their "put-ting on the new man."

St. Louis IX of France, patron of tertiaries, sensed that his Franciscan status grew out of his baptism. He often signed himself "de Poissy," because he had been baptized at that place.

With the Revised Christian Initiation of Adults, the preparation for and conferring of the sacrament or profes-sion of faith has assumed its rightful place, although some-what belatedly in the spiritual lives of believers. The writings and instructions of the early Church stress baptism's importance. At that time, of course, baptism represented a startling break with the past, a conversion to the Gospel, and bearing the injunction of the Lord, "Be perfect as your heavenly Father is perfect." Liturgists claim that infant baptism, a somewhat later practice, was originally the exception. Understanding that baptism remitted all sin and punishment owing to sin, people delayed baptism until later in life to escape the temporal punishment due to sin. It was thought that infants, however, could not invest themselves into the ritual's meaning and effect.

Confirmation was meant to supply for these deficiencies. In the beginning, however, Confirmation was also a sacrament of "initiation." Now, at least in the typical practice of the Church, confirmands have the opportunity to make an adult consecration as, indeed, adult baptism always was. In the Second Letter to the Church at Corinth St. Paul speaks of Christians *separating* themselves from the corruption of this world— "separation" is a crucial aspect of "consecration" or being "set apart." The Apostle wrote, "Since we have these promises, beloved, let us purify ourselves from every defilement of flesh and spirit, and in the fear of God strive to fulfill our consecration perfectly." (II Corinthians 7:1)

Religious profession, including non-vowed Third Order professions, are likewise "consecrations," and they are to be considered analogous with the aforesaid sacraments, especially baptism. Theologians commonly state that on the day of profession one's soul is returned to its pristine state of innocence, so remarkable is the conversion to Jesus by this public act of self-giving and separation from the corruption of the world. Nor does one spontaneously and casually commit oneself to this promised way of life—only one who is called and chosen.

Vocation is a controverted subject. Some will say that professed consecration is for life and dare not be retracted or voided. Others will say that professed consecration may be temporary and after a time of service may be set aside. Beginning with the notion that "vocation" means a "calling," we have to ask "by whom," "to what," and "for how long."

A vocation is a call from proper, legitimate authority. The "calling" authority may be the bishop, the provincial minister, the religious superior, or whoever is empowered and authorized by higher Church government to receive candidates, novices, and professed; to form and educate them; to screen and assess their worthiness; and finally to incorporate them into the body politic of the organization.

During the ordination rite for the diaconate prior to the priesthood—perhaps indicating how the Sacrament of Orders intensifies baptismal commitment—the instruction enjoins celibacy as being "set apart" or consecrated for pastoral charity. Celibacy is a "particular source of apostolic fruitfulness, a special form of consecration and of adherence with 'undivided heart' to Christ."

If this is true of the "calling" authority, one can assume that it is possible to call on a temporary basis for a time of service. Factually that is what happens when a new and potential member professes the organization's way of life for one, two, three, or five years of simple or temporary profession. Hence it is a "given" that temporary consecration (unlike the permanence of baptism) is probable and even necessary in the canonical scheme of things. Nevertheless, we need to emphasize that "separation" and "setting oneself aside" is not transitory, but an enduring status. In the Code of Canon Law early in the twentieth century profession was made once for life. Of course, a person could conceivably leave the organization or get thrown out, but *permanence* was the rubric under which one was vowed, devoted, and consecrated to God.

An ancillary idea of the comparison with baptismal consecration is awareness that one acts in the order of grace, rather than mere nature. Of course, one's proclivities, talents, indeed one's weaknesses and sins, figure into readiness for consecration just as much as one's nature is assessed for baptism. Nevertheless the parameters are those of *grace*. This theological term is used with diverse meanings, from a passing help from God to achieve a noble act to a more-or-less permanent state of being and personhood that bespeaks a relationship with the Three Persons.

When we are said to *grow in grace*, that means our relationship deepens with our Father-Creator, our Brother-Model-Redeemer, and our Spouse-Sanctifier. In baptism this is eminently true, inasmuch as we are given the seven gifts of the Holy Spirit, the theological virtues of faith, hope, and charity, special gifts that fit us for our roles in life, particularly those *charisms* (about which we shall say much more later), such as St. Francis possessed.

I have scarcely brushed the surface of the baptismal gifts, especially the "order of grace," but the analogy with that further consecration which we call "profession" must be fairly clear. The latter intensifies baptism, specifies its Gospel way of life, and makes explicit the triple relationship with the Holy Trinity.

CHAPTER II

Recovering the Franciscan Charism

We read in Chapter Eight of the First Book of Samuel that the elders of Israel approached the prophet and asked him to set a king over them. After all, he was old and his two sons left much to be desired in the judgeship. Even though Yahweh was not entirely pleased, he told Samuel to listen to the voice of the people. Samuel, having no sympathy with the "new breed," warned the Israelites against their "secularism." They wanted to be like other nations. Nevertheless, when the kingship was established, it brought a clearer identity to God's community, and the kings proved to be not notably worse than some of the judges and high priests. The secular tendency and involvement with the world ultimately brought Judaism to its greatest national fruitfulness. Nor did the Jews lose their charism as the chosen people.

Religious orders should remain, like Israel of old, in a constant state of growth and re-formation. Those who possess a charism must be flexible enough to preserve it without obscuring it with the accretions which may merely have been temporary safeguards. In an address to leaders of religious orders on May 23, 1964, Pope Paul VI reminded them that they would remain prosperous only to the degree that their way of life and activities remain under the inspiration of their founders. In 1983 Pope John Paul II wrote of the five foundations of the religious state and warned all the Orders to return to their original charism.

So Dominicans are struggling with the self-concept of contemplative apostles. Carmelites wish to test whether the eremitical life of solitude is consistent with priestly-ministerial labors. The Jesuits are reexamining their function as a missionary institute and creators of small, first-rate liberal arts colleges. Benedictines wonder how stability of place and their origin as a lay movement fit into the mobility of modern life. Assuredly the canonical grant of exemption exists to allow religious institutes to foster their charisms, which the local Ordinary could not be expected to understand in his assignments within the diocese. Some theologians surprisingly wish to make religious priests only members of the diocesan presbyterate. It is alleged that religious orders are at times divisive, since their members move freely from one diocese to another without long-range allegiance to the projects of the local Ordinary. Thus the argument runs that either religious orders of men should be suppressed altogether, or they should be totally controlled in their assignments by the bishop of the diocese. No doubt the Church is best served when religious clergy cooperate closely with and join the diocesan presbyterate for the sake of collegial processes in those areas where religious are affected. But the mission of religious is received uniquely from the Bishop of Rome, who is the focus of the Church's universal mission. Thus even the religious *priests* —not only Sisters and Brothers—need canonical exemption for mobility and service within the Church universal. If religious institutes, particularly those of men, would actually begin to revitalize their mission to the Church, their critics would have less cause to comment with the old cliche that religious take the vows and the diocesan priests observe them. With notable exceptions, however, the "old" religious orders, after a flurry of writing and dialogue for 25 years, have returned to "business as usual," content to let charisms lie buried in history, while they pursue their accustomed and comfortable ministries. The third millennium looks dull, indeed, for religious institutes!

There are not a few scandals or "stumbling blocks" within the three Franciscan Orders as well. The First Order has been divided into three groups, which in some instances are even hostile to one another. The Second Order seemed unable to reconcile divergent elements and splintered into reform groups. The "regular" religious of the Third Order, particularly the Sisters, have not been commonly aware of their share in a specifically Franciscan charism. The "lay" members of the Third Order often cannot find First Order priests to form them into dynamic fraternities. The current solution is to disregard the previous First-Order connections and group all Third-Order fraternities into *regions* instead of *provinces* affiliated with the First Order.

Nevertheless, all three Orders presumably participate in the same renewal of the Christ-life among men that originated with St. Francis of Assisi. He himself remarked, "The Order is a very large society, which is like a worldwide convention joining together in a single life style" (Celano, *Second Life*). One purpose of this study is to clarify the Franciscan charism as the common focus to which all the jurisdictions of the threefold Order can look. Some day charity and flexibility may be so common in the Order that some kind of unity and closer awareness of each other will result. What began as a division within the First Order over involvement with the world or sequestration from it has lost its meaning in the post-

Vatican-II era; involvement is inescapable for active religious. Within each of the Three Orders the life style of one jurisdiction is not unlike the others. And in those few areas where differences are not so minimal, one would think that the Order would be so open a society that the different levels of aspiration could coexist without the multiplication of bureaucracies. What a pity that the Orders splinter in the search for the chimera of "strictness"!

St. Francis was keenly aware of his revolutionary charism (which apparently has been petrified by monastic calcification). "I do not want you to cite me any other rule—not St. Augustine's, nor St. Bernard's, nor St. Benedict's. The Lord told me to become a new type of simpleton in the world. God did not choose to lead me along any other path than the way of experience" (*Legenda Antiqua*). We read in another early biography of his distress over monastic or eremitical currents during his lifetime: "I love my brothers to the degree I am able. Were they to follow my path, I would love them all the more and not alienate myself from them. There are some superiors who are drawing the brothers into different ways after the example of the ancient religious. These men are inattentive to my instructions, but what they are attempting will become obvious in the future" (Celano, *Second Life*) . Perhaps it has taken eight centuries for us to become fully aware of the saint's prediction. For his brothers St. Francis called his Rule their "book of life, the hope of our salvation, the collateral of our glory, the marrow of the Gospel, our way of the cross, the state of perfection, our key to paradise, the guarantee of our eternal testament" (*The Mirror of Perfection*).

Perhaps one explanation of the division within the Order is the ancient Latin aphorism *quot capita tot sententiae*--there are as many opinions about the Franciscan charism as there are persons reflecting upon it. Each concept is likely to spawn a different life style to keep it intact. In each case the problem is to preserve the charism without overwhelming it.

As has been said above, the life style of an Order is related to its charism, or subjective insight, whereby members convalidated their membership within the institutional framework of the Church, which is the normative, objective channel of communication with our heavenly Father. If one does not insist too narrowly upon the analogies, charism and institution are like body and soul, rudder and sail, limits and self-expression. Even within the Order's expression of its charism, a similar polarization tends to develop in order to keep alive and interpret the original life style with precise regulations.

Each institute renews Christ's presence on earth corporately. As every Christian "puts on Christ," so the institute assumes a dimension of the personality of Christ in a way proper to itself. As a social reincarnation of Christ, it becomes a special sign to its lay affiliates or those members of the Mystical Body committed to its spiritual care. Some charisms seem clear: the hermits, the teachers, the nurses, the preachers of Christ crucified, those who orient their lives to the Blessed Sacrament, and so forth. Some institutes seem to have arisen to serve local, sometimes transitory spiritual and social needs. In time they fall into desuetude and perish. For those who have the courage to phase themselves out of existence or merge with others, their "reward in heaven is great" (Matt. 5:12).

Basing themselves, therefore, on the insights of the Founder, Franciscans must specify and clarify their corporate personality or risk losing their identity and perhaps usefulness to the Church and to the world. They must distinguish themselves from foundations which have a similar life style. St. Francis warned St. Clare against those whose teaching or counsel might lead her from her life style and especially from poverty. In his *Testament*, a kind of farewell address to the Order, he once again insisted that the life his brothers were to lead was revealed to him by God alone and was not derived from other religious institutes.

Up to this point, the words "charism," "life style," "religious life," and "corporate personality" have not been precisely differentiated from each other. "Charism" is a general term that indicates a *personal gift* of the Spirit, used for the good of the Church. If it receives approval from the hierarchy, the charism is said to participate in the official mission of the Church to make Christ present in the world. "Religious life" is an "official" charism that represents an *intensified response* of faith to one's baptismal commitment to repeat the life of Christ. "Life style" is the particular *external manifestation* of the Christ-life chosen by an individual or institute. "Personality," finally, refers to the *internal spirit* of the institute, as evidenced by emphasis on certain virtues, certain limits or (conversely) freedom for self-expression, and above all a well-defined self-concept.

One can oppose "personality" to "essence" in defining the spirit of an institute. The latter term is too inflexible, categorized, dogmatic. It is a static statement of the Order's function in the Mystical Body. "Personality," on the other hand, is an existential term. It is a dynamic statement of the Order's place in the Church. "Personality" arises from the insights and experiences of the Order's members. It defines itself according to the perceptions of its members. It admits degrees and potentials not yet specified. This is one of the important principles upon which the rest of these chapters is based.

There is no doubt that the personality of a founder or foundress influences the subsequent evolution of the Order's personality corporately considered. Whereas this is inevitable and even necessary, the two personality concepts are not perfectly interchangeable. Thus the image of St. Francis singing along with the swallows, his hands filled with daisies, and trailed by the rabbits and wolves, is not necessarily compatible with the life style of all his followers. But the freedom to be himself, however silly it might appear to others, is definitely an aspect of St. Francis that is inseparable from his enduring legacy to his sons and daughters, lay or religious. Feel free to own yourself!

An amusing anecdote from the pages of early Franciscan history recalls how the simple Brother Juniper aped St. Francis in such personal habits as coughing when the latter coughed, spitting when he did, and so forth. The annalist made the point, of course, that imitation of the Seraphic saint referred to his spiritual qualities, and prayer life. Whereas no one today is likely so slavishly to copy such actions, even if they were known after a lapse of eight hundred years, the fact remains that St. Francis is not entirely recoverable from history. His biographers used many legends that obscure the facts, always, we may presume, with good will, but in some cases with biased intent. We read dubious accounts of the saint casting a sick brother out of a house he believed some of his confreres had bought, whereas St. Francis shows special concern for the ailing in his Rules. In another account the founder sends Rufino, son of a noble family, naked to preach in the cathedral as a test, whereas St. Francis admonishes his brothers in the Rules not to obey a reprehensible command that would be contrary to their conscience. A story in the *Mirror of Perfection* has St. Francis forbidding a novice to have a breviary for prayer, whereas the Rules specifically allow a breviary. The well-known anthology, *The Little Flowers*, compiled in the fourteenth century, has St. Francis avoiding Elias as a future apostate, whereas Celano's more reliable account of the previous century makes them out to be close friends; in fact, St. Francis appointed Elias the superior of the Holy Land, as well as later of the whole Order.

As is well known, the second generation of Franciscans were divided into several factions according to how they wished to interpret the Rule or Testament of the Founder. The writers who favored certain concepts of poverty or who resisted the structuring process of Brother Elias emphasized and possibly fabricated those stories that supported their claims or interpretations. When St. Bonaventure, the sixth minister general, collected the *Major Legend* between 1260 and 1263 from eyewitnesses who survived the Founder. In the Prologue to the *Major Legend*, St. Bonaventure refers to the *familiaribus eius adhuc superviventibus*. As the Quaracchi Editors show, much of the book derives from Celano's writings. The latter, of course, had an even closer contact than St. Bonaventure with the intimates of St. Francis. In fact, other biographies were no longer allowed to be used, at least officially and in the lessons of the breviary. One purpose of the General Chapter in 1260 at Narbonne was to reconcile those factions in the Order which were publishing slanted writings about St. Francis that supported their personal views. Nevertheless, because of the relative paucity of extraordinary events and miracles in the *Major Legend*, St. Bonaventure was induced to garner and publish other, but possibly less well authenticated stories.

Another case in point is the *Book of Conformities* (circa 1385-1390), attributed to Bartholomew of Pisa and written to cite the parallels between the life of St. Francis and the life of Christ—twelve disciples, the stigmata, and so forth. In fact, it is related that when Donna Pica was about to give birth to the future saint, an angel instructed her to have her child in a stable near their home. This story (upon which medieval piety seems to have nourished itself) has been disproved by the friars' research in Assisi. (Giuseppe Abate, OFM CONV., *La casa dove nacque S. Francesco d'Assisi*, Casa Editrice "Oderisi": Gubbio, 1941).

Nevertheless, such stories are not without value in delineating the personality and life style of the saint. Most of them probably grew from some seeds of truth that reveal the kind of impression St. Francis made upon his contemporaries. The purpose of these chapters is not to sift the historical sources. This has been and is being done by experts. The works of St. Francis himself, published by the Quaracchi College, are the primary source, containing the Rules, *Testament*, and other classical writings. The scholarship and teaching goes on with distinction in Olean, New York at St. Bonaventure University. Nor is it the purpose of this book to prolong the controversies about the true mind of St. Francis, but to offer the writer's opinion about the separability of St. Francis' personality from that of his Order. Perhaps this can serve to bring all Franciscans closer together and provide the Second and Third Orders with a viewpoint on the Franciscan charism which underlies their own approach to God.

Any writer who attempts to distill what is enduring in the personality and life style of St. Francis must be willing to risk the scrutiny of his readers and to expose his own biases and ineptitudes. But the very definition of the "existential personality" as evolving from the members' insights, experiences, and perceptions into potential expressions not yet specified, bespeaks only a tentative blueprint for development. Nevertheless this writer hopes that it is a chart of common aspirations and group objectives, rather than merely one man's opinion.

It is typically the personality combined with his life style which together form a single perception of St. Francis of Assisi that attracts men and women to be his followers. Yet what generally impresses us in the beginning is not what binds us to his charism in the end. One should read a different biography of the saint every year for 10 years after deciding to be his disciple in any of his Three Orders.

Francis was a unique personality and practical innovator. This fact is partly obscured because many of his "new" features on the religious scene have been subsumed into practices and life style common in later religious life. In other words, because such a large percentage of men and women religious today follow his rules of life, his uniqueness in his own day is not at once apparent to us.

For example, Francis sent mobile bands of friars to work in many occupations—not necessarily in apostolates as such (except that they were not to work as foremen or financial managers), but they were assigned to the same friary with ministerially active friars. He taught that what one *does* is less valuable than the *kind of person one is*. One's main achievement, spiritually speaking, lies in *becoming*, not *performing*. There may be a certain arrogance in asserting that there is a Franciscan way of doing everything, if only to show that the Gospel pervades every aspect of every believer's life. Analogously G. K. Chesterton wrote that there is a Catholic way of doing everything, even teaching the alphabet, if only to teach those who learn the alphabet not to despise those who do not (or cannot) learn the alphabet.

In a new way in the Church Francis emphasized the humanness of Christ. He or his followers introduced or popularized the Christmas Crib at Greccio, the Stations of the Cross, the events of the passion, and the ancillary feasts of the Immaculate Conception and St. Joseph later, to cite only a few. The Order's theologians centered on the *humanity* of Christ, but I think Francis centered more profoundly on the *humanness* of Jesus, an altogether different thing, yet the corollary and the crown of "humanity."

"Humaness," whether in Christ or in us, indicates that the whole person is engaged, and that the emotions are important as catalysts in ascertaining and living out values, whether for religious or laity. He wanted his followers to be able to proclaim their love freely to one another. "That we have passed from death to life we know because we love the brothers" and sisters (I John 3:14). We are to express our feelings easily, even the negative ones, as Jesus did, which bespeaks the mature mastery of a persons's emotional life. Our feelings "charge" our actions and give impetus to our projects and attract others to our life style. Most of all, joy makes our spirituality believable, then acceptable.

Even in prayer we use feelings to talk with God, argue or complain, share happiness or show tenderness, fear and anxiety, relief and sorrow. Jesus, too, was angry, wept, was tender, despaired, and experienced betrayal and loneliness.

Other values that are not specifically Franciscan, but are nevertheless part of the Franciscan "career" and "job description," are: 1) loyalty to Christ's Church, its teaching and directives; 2) true sonship and daughterhood of Mary, because no one honored her more than Jesus; 3) accepting sufferings and reverses to identify with Jesus and the poor and disenfranchised, while remaining content; 4) always reading the Gospel as normative; 5) bonding with like-minded members of the Franciscan movement. I say these values are not "specifically Franciscan," even though they are honored by all followers of Francis, who cherished these values in his life, but other believers, particularly earlier religious Orders, revered the Gospel, cherished Mary, and so forth.

Note that all of the above requires us who do not know the future to *live tentatively*, asking for enough grace faithfully to live "until midnight today," *not clinging* to anything from this passing world, but especially our own will and our favorite projects. Not always being able to be very noble and holy, we remember that we are not called to success (because our "success" and God's may not be the same), but to struggle. We are called not to specific achievements, but hopefully to all possible achievements and to constant preparation for them. Although Franciscans long for a safe harbor, God expects them to voyage at risk.

This last is attested to by the annual harvest of biographies about the Founder and the proliferation of new Franciscan foundations and the centuries-long vigor of the Third Order of St. Francis, which has inherited all that has been written in this chapter. Even now believers and cynics find no fault with the saint, who remains an anomaly today as the one who longed to suffer more, endure more, and joyfully possess less than any person alive, without ever making deprivation an end in itself. He released himself from the status-seeking of his time, the pressures of his father and peers, and the expectations of the Church. One expression of his emotional life and humanness was his delight in romanticism, calling himself the "herald of the Great King," "the trouba-dour of Christ," and "the knight of the Most High." An-other expression was his love and respect for nature, so simple and unspoiled because it obeyed God's commands—the sun to ripen the fruit, the birds to give their morning concert, and the flowers to carpet the valleys with color. He evoked his own sensitivity and ours by writing the Canticle of Brother Sun in the newly-discovered Italian vernacular.

In tracing the origin and definition of the Franciscan charism the humanness of Christ is paramount. In fact, we study St. Francis only to follow Christ more closely. It would be a travesty to see Francis in isolation and forget he was early on called "the Christ of Umbria." It is a fair historical judgment that St. Francis wished to restore the world to the springtime of the Church. All three of the Founder's Orders were meant to recover the primitive Christian experience, as we read in the Acts of the Apostles.

Nevertheless one cannot understand Franciscanism as an historical movement only in the light of the first century, because St. Francis was a child of his time and culture, as in geography, asceticism, and technology. Yet he wanted his followers to have sign-value for all times. He said the Order was given to the world for its salvation. He was conscious of the subtlety of God's design for human history, which was meant to be a love story, not a legal contract, not based on fear, but transformation into Christ, not meant for an elitist and select group, but for all who accept the Gospel as com-mon property. He was not trying to create a "safe environ-ment" for his followers, just as at the Last Supper Jesus told his Father not to remove his disciples from this world. De-spite some non-negotiable rules, he left his followers free to listen to the voice of the Spirit. In his "revival" of Christian-ity, Francis projected a communitarian enterprise. As St. Maximilian Kolbe said often that "hate destroys, love alone creates," so St. Francis would say "love is inventive—for oth-ers."

To the end of his life St. Francis was refining his self-concept and understanding of Jesus. On a birthday towards the end of his life, he turned to his brothers and plaintively asked, "When will we *begin* to serve the Lord? Up to this time we have done nothing." He always was suspicious of documents and forbade his followers to seek written permissions from Church authority. He liked Gospel maxims, but eschewed written rules for many years. If one loved enough, laws would be irrelevant; when laws are left unwritten, one goes much further in fulfilling them. Look at the Gospel imperatives: Go beyond the restriction of poverty—hold loosely in your hand whatever is not of eternal value, for it is useless. Go beyond the restriction of chastity—love all others and God most of all. Go beyond the restriction of obedience—submit to another for the sake of him who was obedient unto death. In other words, Franciscans embrace a way of life, an attitude, but mostly a Person, not a set of legal documents.

Legends need to be sifted and judged and separated from history if possible, so the "true" St. Francis might emerge. Yet perhaps all the stories contain some truth. He forbade his First Order friars to enter the monasteries of women and to have suspicious contacts with women. But he asked Lady Giacoma Settesoli to be present at his death bed and frequently visited her in Rome. She is interred at the end of the chapel opposite the bones of the Founder in Assisi. He resisted writing the Rule, but he called it the marrow of the Gospel and key to eternal life. Nevertheless, St. Francis was more concerned about his followers' inner disposition than outer conformity to a directive. A careful reading of the Rule of 1223 confirms this outlook. As the Lord pronounced many important spiritual directives with the preface, "Amen, amen, I say to you," so Francis a few times in his rule prefaces a piece of counsel (rather than a regulation) with the preface, "I admonish and exhort the brothers," as regarding preaching and public conduct. For example, in Chapter 10 he said, "I admonish and exhort the friars to avoid all pride, empty glory, envy, avarice, worry, and anxiety over this world, and detraction, and murmuring."

We have all known men and women Franciscans who placed their holiness not in the heart, but the letter of the law. Or perhaps they mistook St. Paul's statement that Christian law is written on the fleshy tablets of the heart! So they stumble over every syllable of the breviary, the consecratory formula of the Mass, and sacramental rites instead of speaking naturally and in a human way. And their asceticism is no joyful assumption of mortification, but a careful recording of sins and temptations. With sterile lives they go about the world to make disciples just as rigid as they are! We fail unless we show that holiness is possible, as the Founder showed that the Gospel is livable.

Just two and a half years before he died, in his *Letter to a General Chapter* just before the Pentecost Chapter of 1224, Francis still cited his need for conversion on his spiritual journey. "I have sinned in many ways through my own most grievous fault, particularly in not keeping the Rule I promised to God, and in not saying the office as the Rule prescribes, due to carelessness or sickness, or because I am ignorant and never studied." This was not the attitude of a beginner on the purgative way, but his lifelong concept of kenosis, or emptying himself out. This was not merely a sign of his creatureliness. He was constantly being uprooted from the City of Man to be replanted in the fertile soil of the City of God.

St. Francis did not want to judge his society except indirectly by proposing another plan of values. He did not want the vowed life to be an indictment of the "world." Money, sex, and power ploys (opposed to the evangelical counsels or vows) are never evil in themselves; they are legitimate human pursuits if they are moral and honorable. Hence Franciscans and all religious persons serve as measuring sticks of spiritual values for the world.

Similarly Francis stood at the edge of medieval society, looking inside neither wistfully nor enviously, but as one seeing through and beyond it. Jesus had the same predilection for marginated people, tax-collectors, prostitutes, lepers, and Samaritans. Why was this important to Jesus and Francis? It was because one of the signs of the coming of the Messianic Kingdom is that the poor and disadvantaged have the Gospel preached to them. We live in an age of transition, the end of the second millenium of Christianity, when convenience and expedience form our ethics, manipulation and exploitation are our politcs, wealth and fame give the hallmark of human success and a kind of immortality.

If St. Francis were alive today, his charism would appear differently in its externals. He could not find wolves to tame and birds to preach to in our downtown cities. I don't know whether he'd get the Nobel Peace Prize or appear on evening television talk shows. But he would insist that we stand against our times and take the Gospel at the full and really trust God rather than the government. Francis would tell us to accept the crosses we cannot reasonably escape and emphasize the Spirit over legislation and policies. He would counsel us to trust our emotions if their context is customary self-discipline, and trust our humanness over bureaucracy. Prefer the poor, he would tell us; realize your effectiveness derives from grace, not your effort. Finally, he would assert, love the Church in order to preserve the community of faith. The Franciscan charism leads in these directions.

CHAPTER III

History as a Conditioner of Charism

The term "history" is used here in a twofold sense. A person develops within the unique milieu of the emotional tone of his home life, the structure of his family, his developmental rate, his personal education, the traumatic events of his youth, and so on. Secondly, a person is the product of his times, its politics, its prejudices, its superstitions, its peculiar ethos.

The personal history of St. Francis brings to mind his flair for the dramatic, a decidedly romantic view of life, a desire to be his "own man" against the options of his father, and, no doubt, some grandiose ideas of his own future greatness—all of which, had he failed, would have provided just another case in a psychology text. It is important to analyze these factors in his personality in order to compare them with the "existential personality" of his foundation, the three Orders and their subdivisions.

It took many sober confrontations with hunger, mockery, and alienation from his fellows to make Francis more realistic. Nevertheless he did not lose his gaiety, freedom of expression, and aspiration to change the whole world. When theoreticians dissect a saint's life in behavioristic or psychoanalytic literature, they provide a real service to those who follow the saint, even if some of their underlying theoretical models have to be rejected. Whereas these personal case studies are invaluable, there is always the peril that a vocation might be reduced to a merely natural phenomenon. A vocation, however—an inexplicable mystery—is also a supernatural gift. A charism cannot be quantified; it is more (at least to the believer) than a career choice, although it is also that, inasmuch as a charism can be rejected because of a human agent's inaccessibility to the Spirit. A vocational charism is a profound and continuing engagement of the person with God; it is locked up in that rapport which is the communication of the self—both the divine and the human self. People who have been in love can understand. Nevertheless, to the degree that the ego needs of a person can be scrutinized, the natural processes bound up in a charism are subject to description.

Throughout the history of the mystical life of the community of God, we see that certain qualities are attributed to certain saints, not only inseparably from their names, but also as if their heroic virtue had been founded upon a particular quality. There was the seraphic St. Teresa of Avila, the soldierly St. Ignatius Loyola, the serene St. Francis de Sales, the "little" St. Therese of Lisieux, the chaste St. Aloysius, the poor and humble Man of Assisi. As the theologians like to assert, the possession of one virtue to a heroic degree perforce includes all the others. Whereas such heroism may, indeed, be a legacy to a saint's followers, one cannot assume that a single virtue is the totality of a charism handed on to a whole religious institute. Each saint presumably practices all the virtues as occasions present themselves and according to the level of his spiritual development.

Before applying these ideas to the personality of St. Francis, it is necessary to comment on a broader historical context of a person's philosophy of life. As the Roman annalist Tacitus succinctly remarked in his classic epigram: "Strengths of character are most accurately measured in the light of the era which most easily gave them rise."

The *theological background* of a saint may give him a prejudice as easily as an insight. It is said that St. Francis Xavier told the Japanese that their ancestors were in hell. When St. Francis of Assisi wrote his *First Rule*, containing his authentic thought, he directed his missionary brothers to avoid contentions and disputes and to be subject to every human being. Then they were to announce the word of God, if it appeared pleasing to the Lord. When the five protomartyrs of the Order preached in North Africa, apparently they announced that Mohammed and his followers were the minions of the devil—which is not a very ecumenical observation. We remember that St. Paul the Apostle himself had to revise his thinking as he slowly realized that he was not, after all, living in the last few years of the Church with Christ's reappearance imminent.

A saint's personal *asceticism* reflects a relationship to the existing economic level or standard of living. Self-discipline must be more stringent than the average way of life to count for mortification. Yet the lower middle classes of the twentieth century—or even many of the poor receiving public aid—live in greater abundance, variety, and physical security than the wealthy of the twelfth century. Asceticism, therefore, may not be wholly interpreted outside the reference to its historical milieu and the customs of the time. Above all, asceticism has no meaning outside the context of its motivation, which can change from century to century.

The *scientific knowledge* of an age tends to color its philosophical currents. Thus the Middle Ages were distrustful of tampering with nature or delving into such "diabolical" arts. Even the good Franciscan Roger Bacon was imprisoned for experiments common today in grammar school. Past concepts of geography so limited men's horizons that during the medieval period, for example, missionary ventures to dim, distant lands seemed unimportant or impossible—at least prior to Franciscan and Dominican excursions to Tartary even before the Polos. In our own time we see religious persons eschew the findings of the behavioral sciences that can aid spiritual and psychological maturation. The scientific study of ancient literatures, religions of the world, and anthropology casts light upon the meanings of Sacred Scripture that otherwise knowledgeable and religious men and women are reluctant to accept.

The *political and nationalistic tendencie ss* of some eras left their mark also on religious Orders. Up to our own time we read the constitutions of some Orders which exclude Catholics of Jewish extraction from entering their ranks without demeaning "dispensations." Monarchical structures that smack of the "divine right of kings" and militaristic regimes that form members into unthinking robots who plant cabbages upside down at a command have fostered a concept of law that reflected the thinking of the leaders rather than the aspirations of all the members.

The *personal idiosyncrasies* of a founder or saint often rise out of his environment. Some considered bathing too sensual, halitosis a sign of an evil interior disposition, and any kind of humor an insult to the suffering Christ (of whom it is not recorded in the Gospel that he ever laughed). One would not cavil, of course, at St. Paul of the Cross, who wore no hat out of respect for the omnipresent God—if the story is true—because he did not impose his personal asceticism upon his followers. Also, the forms of prayer and meditation that succeeded for a foundress may have been bequeathed to subsequent generations of followers, simply because they were commonly accepted norms in a past century. The accretions of the *devotio moderna* are a case in point. Some types of Marian devotion, a certain sentimentality in prayers, and sacred art forms that distract rather than edify are examples of other personal viewpoints that can be thrust upon a whole institute. To all these environmental factors that condition a religious founder must be added the human ones: spiritual directors who may have been insensitive to the nature of the charism, manipulatory bishops and pastors who needed personnel fo fill a local need not related to the charism, and the influence upon a founder or foundress who lived temporarily with an already existing religious institute.

The melodramatic dimension of St. Francis' personality, for example, caused him to strip before the townspeople of Assisi and return even his clothes to his natural father, so that thereafter he might call God alone his father. Another time he expressed a desire to have even the walls of houses smeared with meat on Christmas, so that they might "feast" in commemoration of the Lord's birth. He directed his brothers to collect any scrap on which the name of the Lord had been written and discarded, lest it be walked upon. The General Chapter, however, countermanded St. Francis. It is shallow theology lightly to attribute such actions—assuming they are all historical events—to the indwelling Spirit of a saint.

In any case, these excesses were on the periphery of St. Francis' personality and do not represent a significant dimension of his life any more than the odd actions every human being occasionally performs. These extraordinary acts were relatively rare in St. Francis' life when set into the broad sweep of his life style. Such things are not essential to following him, except insofar as they reveal a transparent and spontaneous person who was not fearful of exposing his emotional life. They appear in the literature for the obvious reason that such material makes better reading than the daily, monotonous, earthbound commitment to prayer, work, and normal asceticism.

This distinction must be made in the personality of St. Francis as well as in the struggle of the first Franciscans to achieve a corporate identity or charism. For example, St. Francis gave St. Anthony permission to study and teach the brothers sacred theology. This must have presumed a desire for learning on their part, even though St. Francis in his *Second Rule* warns the unlettered brothers not to be *anxious* to acquire learning. Later on, St.Bonaventure's theological work *De reductione omnium artium ad theologiam* subsumes all human learning under some aspect of sacred science. As the Order continues to clarify its self-concept by its activities in the third millenium of Christianity, it will continue to research the theological dimension of psychology, literature, science, the cinema, and so forth. Yet St. Francis might have forbidden analogous activities to his contemporary brothers.

We see history affecting other divisions of Franciscandom as well. Tertiaries at one time took vows even though they lived with their families. Unfortunately this appeared too fluid a state for religious life in the minds of the hierarchy, and as time passed, the secular Third Order became in effect another of countless parochial organizations. The monasticizing of the Poor Clares is another case close at hand. It seems to be alien to the Franciscan spirit to prevent truly human engagement and apostolic availability by placing curtains and grilles between the Clares and visitors or clients of the household. It is appalling to realize that, except for those Second Order convents which are beginning to adapt, a member can go to the parlor to visit only in the presence of another Sister; that she can never give her family a kiss and embrace; that she is not even allowed to see others' faces. This was certainly not the life style between St. Francis and St. Clare themselves. The Rule of the Poor Clares was approved on August 9, 1253, by Pope Innocent IV. But St. Francis never wrote a Rule for them himself; it was as if he were yet trying to determine a life style consonant with the Gospel. Perhaps he could not reconcile the strict enclosure that women typically experienced with his own free spirit. Nevertheless he wholeheartedly approved the Poor Clares' poverty as compared with the wealth of some women's monasteries.

Even for his own brothers St. Francis wrote two Rules. Some scholars refer to the *three* Rules of St. Francis. The first, however, was merely a collection of Scriptural quotations. Francis thought that the Bible was a sufficient guide for a friar. He was pressed later to comment. The "second" Rule was a lengthy compilation of bible texts. Finally the "third" Rule (in 1223, commonly referred to as the Second Rule or Bullata) was more manageable, if somewhat more legalistic.

CHAPTER IV

The First Franciscan

St. Francis lived in an age of growing materialism. Historians may have overdrawn the corruption of the diocesan priesthood, the withdrawal of monks from the arena of the world, and the spiritual indifference of lay Catholics, in order to contrast the saint more sharply with his times. Nevertheless, it was certainly a fact that the age was torn by wars, communes were asserting independence from feudal lords, the wealth of monasteries seemed to have little in common with the poor. Usurious practices, the attitude of the newly rising merchant classes, and the seeking of benefices by the clergy did not reflect the principles of the Gospel. The *minores*, or lower classes, whom we would call the disenfranchised today, were only second-rate citizens, without full civil rights. The institutional Church was unable to cope with a situation for which it was also responsible in part. So the Holy Spirit breathed a new charism into the

Church through the instrumentality of the Man from Assisi.

This was a man who led no armies, except the spiritual shock troops of a new movement. He wrote no profound or scholarly works, only a few letters and the Rules which he called the marrow of the Gospel. His financial empire was grounded on the providence of God and the economy of poverty. He was an unprepossessing figure, rather homely, of a slight build unfit for athletic honors, save in running the good race and winning the laurel of divine glory. He developed no theory of personality or theraputic psychology, but simply proposed an example of the imitation of Christ as a panacea for man's problems.

On the other hand, St. Francis did not reject the Establishment. He did not denounce the generals, the scholars, the financiers, the athletes, and the ill-starred reformers of his day. He rather owned up to his own weaknesses. I suspect he would not have denounced communism as a political theory (aside from its atheism and violent revolutions), but would have rejoiced that whole nations were idealistically attempting to "share everything in common," as we read of the early Christians (Acts 2: 44). The social dropouts, who hold him as a kind of patron saint, would not have been condemned for their odd rejection of the world's values. But St. Francis would have offered them his alternate plan to change the world's values.

The growth that preceded his total decision for Christ was drawn out for several years. He lived in confusion and in alienation from men and women he had cherished in his earlier life, but he kept faith that his Master would provide a better friendship. A leap from one sort of life into another wholly unlike it was precarious for him as well as it would be for any man. That divine grace is present does not mean that the human struggle is absent; the one generally triggers the other. Each added insight was born of lonely relfection upon himself. He was a pragmatic person, who knew that, if others were to have faith in his mission, they would have to see that kind of knowledge which is experience. As he was later quoted in the *Mirror of Perfection*: "A person possesses no more knowledge than what is put to practice, just as a religious is a preacher only according to the measure of his actions. The tree is known only by its fruits."

His illness in the jail of Perugia taught Francis the brevity of life. His fever and vision on the road to battle showed him that he was to serve the Lord God, not a warlord. The high life of Assisi, to which he momentarily returned, demonstrated the emptiness of a life lived for pleasure. The months of moody isolation in a cave outside of town led him to abandon himself to the only Caretaker who would not fail to provide every essential need for life here and hereafter. Seeking out beggars to imitate and lepers to kiss tested the degree of his self-conquest. The taunts of the community and ire of his father reinforced his willingness to suffer the supreme test of his ego, which is the ridicule from those to whom we have exposed our inner convictions and our emotional life. The simplicity with which he was to live out his dream is attested to by the unstudied way in which he accepted the mandate to rebuild San Damiano, not yet aware that the Crucified had a larger task of reconstruction planned for him.

As the chronicler records of this long process of growth, St. Francis began to value himself less. This was not in the sense of despising himself, which can be a sickness as easily as a virtue. For he confidently begged alms, collected stones, and invited others to pay with sweat, as he jocosely said, for rebuilding the Church. Finally at the age of twenty-six, on February 24, 1208, he was startled to hear the Gospel of the feast of St. Matthias as if he had heard it for the first time. "The reign of God is at hand!" (Cf. Matt. 10:7-13.)

In his psychoanalytical study of the Protestant reformer Martin Luther, Erik H. Erikson, *Young Man Luther* (New York: Norton, 1962, page 44), Erik Erikson points out how creative persons decree a moratorium for themselves, as it were. Their inner selves are cultivated while they often starve themselves socially, erotically, and even nutritionally. Young man Francis did this same thing when he lived in a cave near Assisi. He went to Rome and exchanged clothes with a beggar to test his ability to identify with the poor. He served lepers and the outcasts of society as a means of starving his sense life, to which he had formerly granted indulgence. This occurred between 1206 and 1208. Meanwhile his father grew more exasperated and his mother more distraught at the fool they had brought into the world.

This starvation and moratorium were as necessary as the poise for balance on a springboard before a perilous high dive. Was this to be another failure? First he had renounced a merchant's career. His businessman father grumbled, but, reliving his own apparently lackluster life in his son's adventures, fitted him out for war. Off the boy went in the spring of 1205 to join Gauthier of Palearis, the Chancellor of Emperor Frederick II, in his wars of succession to the Neapolitan states. When he came back home, tried the party circuit again, and finally crawled away from life into a cave, any parent would have been more than dyspeptic—history has dealt too severely with Pietro Bernardone, the father of St. Francis.

Erik Erikson has drawn the lines of the Oedipal conflict very sharply in the life of Martin Luther. He shows how the elder Luther's arbitrary punishments and imposition of personal goals upon his sone were later reflected in the thinking of Luther the theologian. God the Father cannot be pleased by human endeavor; all that human beings can do is blindly believe that the incomprehensible "mood swings" of a father somehow are based on compassion. Luther himself records that he almost ran away from the celebration of his first Mass when, at the beginning of the Canon, he had to address God the Father directly and without a mediating person. The reader is directed to pages 58, 138, and 221 of Erickson's fascinating book.

Although many influential men of history give evidence of an Oedipal conflict, the altercation between Pietro and Francis does not seem to fall into this category. It is true that his mother, Donna Pica, lavished abundant affection on the boy. We read that once she released him from the cellar-prison in their home, where his father had confined him during one of his angry episodes. Whether one could conclude that this mother-relationship (opposed, incidentally, by the elder Luther in *his* home) occasioned a tender regard for the Mother of God on St. Francis' part later in life is rather arbitrary. In any case, during the childhood, adolescence, and young manhood of our saint, his father gave both financial and emotional support and approval to his son. Unlike Martin Luther, the reformer Francis had no need or desire to challenge the authority of the Church. Further, so accustomed to a happy and consistent relationship with his natural father when he was growing up, St. Francis readily transferred his feelings to his supernatural Father. He was not so self-confident during his personal "moratorium," as might be expected; when he lost his father's good graces, he asked an elderly beggar who accompanied him through Assisi, to bless him if he by chance encountered his father's curses. This symbolic action was useful until he *experienced* the divine fatherliness and could say before the world that having only a Father in heaven sufficed for him. Because of his great joy in religious life, there was no "credibility gap" to his statement.

It is the nature of Christian virtue to consist in a struggle. It is not the quality of heroic virtue to have one's will and senses dead to provocation, but to have them oriented to what is positive, morally acceptable, and even enjoyable. Striking this balance with heroic vigilance is the heart of virtue. Thus St. John of the Cross accurately commented toward the end of his life that his extreme sense-deprivations had so become a way of life that they lost the quality of a virtue. St. Francis seems to have had a "sword of Damocles" hanging over head all his life, bearing witness to his heroic struggle. Once when erotic thoughts provoked him, he threw himself into the briers. Another time he built figures of a "wife" and "children" in the snow with the comment to his confreres that he might beget children yet if he did not continue the struggle.

Physical ills occurred several times in St. Francis' life, exacerbated by his own fasts and irregular life. His fevers from the abortive military exploit to Perugia, his hemorrhages and ulcers toward the end of his life, his failing eyesight which some physician tried to cure with hot irons, his possible cancer that may have ended his life in his middle forties—these were contributory to a state of health that must have affected his psychological life as well. Biographers mention that "demons" drove him to despair by whispering that there would be no salvation for one who ruined his health with excessive mortification. Later in his life the saint complained that he was beset by devils. When he was at prayer by himself on one occasion, he fancied that someone was creeping up behind him to watch. He imagined that voices shrieked out to him in mockery during mountain storms. He had nightmares of a devil who told him that all was in vain, because Francis would finally belong to him anyway. We cannot tell if these episodes of depression were frequent in the life of a man characterized by his contemporaries as consistently joyful and alert to life. It may be that medieval biographers seized upon the episodes as dramatic and sensational anecdotes. In any case, depressions occur to the best of men; how they handle them is more revelatory of psychic life than that they occur. But they cannot be overlooked in delineating the personality of a saint.

Many of the experiences of young man Francis affected the expression of his charism. When he was still working in his father's shop, he once turned away a beggar who asked an alms for the love of God, because he was in the midst of a sale. He was so ashamed that he ran after the beggar with a generous donation. Later he instructed the brothers never to refuse a request made in the name of the love of God. In his

First Rule, Chapters Seven and Eight, he set down as law what were really personal clarifications of his charism that he left out of the *Second Rule.* He commanded his confreres to receive robbers and thieves into the friary; he had done so with a remarkable change in their lives, even to the point of some joining the Order. He permitted the brothers to collect money for their sick members, since he himself had been so plagued by illnesses. In the *Second Rule,* however, he reiterated the command to care for the sick brothers, but forbade the taking of money for any reason. He likewise mentions concern for lepers in the *First Rule*—which is a consequence of his personal experiences. This does not appear in the *Second Rule.* The latter is not shorter in the number of prescriptions, as a matter of fact; but, rather, the *First Rule* is longer because of the lengthy prayers and quotations from the Scriptures. If St. Francis had lived for another ten years, he might have helped his nascent Order to specify its charism even further. Perhaps he would have completed a written rule of life of the Clares and the tertiaries.

The "moratorium" of St. Francis—if not the heroic struggle—ended at the Church of St. Nicholas, April 15, 1208. For a month and a half he had worn a peasant's tunic. He had received his first two confreres. He still had no intention of establishing a religious congregation; his was a simple trio of laymen. In a fashion that makes us uneasy, but in keeping with a medieval practice of discerning God's will or prophesying the future by opening the pages of Scripture or of Virgil's works, the three opened the Gospel book at St. Nicholas three times. If they wanted to be perfect, they had to sell all that they had and give it to the poor. They were to take nothing on their proposed venture. They had to deny themselves in order to follow Christ. It is interesting to observe that the three passages do not actually provide a positive prescription at all. The brothers were told to divest themselves of encumbrances. The life style and "personality" of their charism still had to be researched by experiential knowledge. One can easily apply these same three prescriptions to a monk, a hermit, a canon regular, a consecrated virgin, a layman, and so forth.

Despite St. Francis' own ambivalences, he always maintained that the source of his experience was divine. "As the Lord has truthfully revealed to me, God is going to make us thrive into a great congregation and expand our numbers to the uttermost parts of the earth. For your own good," he told his confrerers, "I am constrained to show you what I have seen. Nevertheless I would rather keep silence in this matter, had charity not forced me to tell it to you" (Celano, *First Life*). When he reminisced in his final *Testament*, he reiterated, "After the Lord gave me some brothers, nobody pointed out what I should do. But the Most High himself revealed to me that I should live according the the pattern of the holy Gospel." Insofar as the Scriptures provide the source and inspiration for St. Francis, his innovations are rather to be considered a restoration to a world that had forgotten them.

I confess I have little liking or sympathy for many of the saccharine biographies of St. Francis, replete with poetic phrases and "sweet fancies." Here we have a manly soldier of God, a prisoner in the Perugia dungeon, a patient with illness most of his life, no stranger to despair and disaffection, alienated from and alienating those he was supposed to love most on earth, ignorant of learning, at the age of 26 not knowing what he was going to do when he grew up.

Here was a "loser," however lovable he might be, even across the centuries. In the end he was rejected even by his followers, members of his own Order. But even this last was consonant with his following of Jesus. To all outward appearances Jesus, too, was a "loser." Consider how he was degraded, betrayed, denied, deserted by those he had loved and taught in close harmony for three years. He died as a criminal on a cross of shame, in fact, considered as a heretic for his theology. One cannot understand Francis outside the context of his embracing the life and death of Jesus, content to be a "loser" in the world's eyes.

Franciscans seem always to be anxious to bring a common message about their founder's charism to the world. But nothing could be farther from the truth. Is the "proper" follower of the saint the friar who preaches middle-class values? Or the layperson who attends all the Secular Franciscan meetings and recites the required prayers? Or the Poor Clare who lives quietly in her cloister while longing for news of the "outside world"? Or the prayerful contemplative hermit who runs from contact with the "world"? Or the businessman or professional or priest who enjoys the world's technology and surrounds himself or herself with the best stereo systems and entertainment center?

The "common" message with respect to the founder is that the message is always uncommon, personal, unique, proper to the individual who perceives Francis. The point of dialogue is to see the other's point of view without necessarily accepting the vision and the dream and the journey and entry into the Kingdom. Which Francis is to be announced to the world? A review of the biographies of St. Francis indicates the biases and prejudices of most authors, their contradictions and misconceptions.

My own prejudices make me lean toward the following: G. K. Chesterson for a literary feast, Arnaldo Fortini, the former mayor of Assisi, for a comprehensive background about the saint, and Omer Englebert for a straightforward life of the founder. I never found anyone, especially scholars, who proposed absolutely and fervently a single volume about Francis of Assisi.

Looking at Francis as the "glorious leader" of the Order, we first point out that the leader should know and present the group task best—at least, better than any member. If prayer, humanness, emotional transparency, clarity of vision, etc. are intrinsic to a Franciscan leader, man or woman, then

Francis' name leads all the rest. It is said further that every "institution is the lengthened shadow of one person," usually the founder or director or C. E. O. This is a mixed blessing. The overwhelming, lingering presence of a single person can be stultifying and inhibitory, because sometimes a single mold is the only one acceptable and newcomers are made into *clones*. This is the major difficulty in vocation recruitment today, probably for all religious Orders. The so-called vocation director manipulates the candidates into clones, generally of himself. If that director is also in formation, the problem is compounded. If the vocation director has a penchant to be "macho," then a simple, gentle soul will find no place in the fraternity. If the director is a weakling, he will be intimidated by a manly, aggressive candidate and will find many excuses to put off the potential member.

What is the point? *Freedom in the Spirit* is the point. The principal formator is the Holy Spirit who forms every believer into Christ. The Spirit liberates because It "breathes where it wills." It leads every individual to holiness according to a divine plan, not a vocation director's scheme. Candidates leave because they grow discouraged at not being allowed to "bloom" where they are planted. Franciscans cannot grow without freedom, because that is an implicit quality of the charism voiced and expressed by the founder. There are always some rules and regulations for friars or laypersons or sisters—simply for good order, yet freedom is the rubric under which the *Rule* and *Constitutions* are embraced, otherwise one is ultimately reduced to slavery!

St. Francis' power over us is not that of a superior enforcing laws we must obey, but that of a teacher. Note that Jesus in the Gospels did not exert the power and authority which he truly always possessed from his Father. As John E. Dalberg, Lord Acton, wrote to Bishop Mandell (1887), "Power tends to corrupt; absolute power corrupts absolutely." Francis did not seek this kind of power. For example, he insisted on having a Cardinal Protector as supervisor of his Order and liaison with the Holy See. He required absolute obedience to the Pope. He did not allow his brothers to preach in dioceses of reluctant or hostile bishops. As for himself, the faithful imitator of Jesus, Francis did not choose to exercise *power* as such, but in his teacher-model role, he wanted *influence* or persuasion over his followers. I have taken note in my life that there is an inverse proportion between power (authority) and influence (persuasiveness). The more you "get" or are given or achieve of the one reduces the effective presence of the other. (The day I was elected minister provincial was the day I seemed to lose influence over my confreres. After leaving office the situation reversed a little.) I think that when the young Franciscan Order passed from the patriarchal to the senatorial form of government, the founder remained the spiritual focus as the power slipped through his fingers.

As he lay dying, he must have thought of what kind of teacher he had been. A wise man claimed that a true teacher guides his students' eyes away from himself to the spirit that quickens or motivates him. St. Francis was a master of such persuasion. He did not seek a personal entourage to be his fan club, although that seemed to happen anyway. He was always leading them to the imitation of Jesus as discovered in theGospel, his charism. Some leaders loom so large over their institutions that they dwarf their followers. The great "giant leaders" bring their followers into gianthood. In other words, the truly great giant gets out of the way of the Holy Spirit. St. Francis turned his students' eyes to the quickening of the Spirit of Truth which liberates the followers to be become all they can be in truth. I remember the powerful words of Francis Bacon writing *On Truth*, "No pleasure is comparable to standing upon the vantage ground of truth" and judging everything one sees according to that truth. "You shall know the truth and the truth shall set you free."

Perhaps the greatest tribute a friar, sister, or layperson can pay to the first Franciscan is to grow to the point where you no longer need him (or his visible presence) because you no longer need to strive consciously for his attributes, inasmuch as imitation of Christ through Francis has become a second nature. Each Franciscan becomes in his or her turn a "new kind of simpleton in this world"—and simpletons are notably individualistic, idiosyncratic, and invested with a personal spirit and inner truth that sets them free!

Cicero would have choked on Francis' Latin; Virgil would not be impressed by the "Canticle of Brother Sun." Roman canonists stumbled on his optimistic imprudence. But an artist would have understood when he encapsulated an emotion or religious insight concretely—in a scrap of music, play-acting, poetical images. He put on beggar's clothes in Rome to see "how it felt to beg in the piazza." He tore up a page of the New Testament so the unlettered brothers could have a piece to press to their heart. He set words about loving God to hit songs of the streets (as our national anthem was originally set to a popular love song). He enacted paraliturgies for Christmas at Greccio and Calvary when he received the stigmata on La Verna. He bought a lamb being taken for slaughter as he recalled the Lamb of God. He nursed lepers because their lesions were the wounds of Christ. When he played the clown and barefoot troubadour and knight of the Most High, the role he was playing was somehow Jesus Christ, the Suffering Servant, who emptied himself out and embraced the status of a slave. When he rescued a worm in danger of being trampled on the roadway, he accepted brotherhood with creation and recalled the "ultimate gesture of cosmic humility": the Incarnation as a fellow human by God's own Son.

The charism of Francis summons us to relive the life of Jesus, to make the City of God and of Man into one dwelling place, not to bring the Lord to the City but proclaim that he is already there, so the springtime of the Church might bloom again. We recall a simpler time of the world or, more importantly, of our own lives when everything was clear, our vision was unclouded about our vocation, and the path to heaven uncluttered because the irrelevant was lasered away by our hot zeal. Perhaps this is the history of the whole Church, not just the Franciscan Order. Each Franciscan passes through early fervor, then a period of inconstancy and mediocrity, during which the person "settles in" and settles for modest holiness (if such a thing exists!). This is the typical way of all flesh. By grace alone with dogged perseverance one can recover the first, simpler ideal and step in line behind the galaxy of saints—and be counted as an honest follower of Francis.

In that never-ending struggle between charism and authority the Gospel cedes to Canon Law; the *Rule* of the founder multiplies into reams of *Constitutions* and *Statutes*. In the same town where the saint begged stones and a donation of sweat, throngs of workmen and paid artisans erected basilicas to honor the Little Poor Man. By that time neither his bones nor his charism belonged to him or his Order. The grand churches at the Sacro Convento and Portiuncula memorialize this. The founder belongs to the world.

Jesus' great lesson to us as he died is forgiveness—"who but God can forgive sin?" He knew his disciples would run; they had already quarreled for the places of honor; they remained earthbound and pedestrian. But Jesus looked to their forgiveness; by his lowly service of washing their feet he anticipates their total cleansing from sin. The central service of Jesus is the praise of his heavenly Father and the healing forgiveness of his brothers and sisters on earth. At Bethlehem we heard, "Glory to God in the highest, and peace on earth to men of good will." This sums up everything in Jesus' life, and Francis repeated the experience of the Lord.

They ended up "liminal" persons standing at the threshold, yet excluded from their kingdoms, outcasts. The followers of St. Francis are given to the world for its healing and forgiveness, to wash its feet, love its unlovable, forgive its unforgivable, even cherish its ugliness.

To praise Francis without imitation is empty flattery.

CHAPTER V

St. Francis' Creative Expression of Religious Life

Three factors in St. Francis' personality tend to rise to the surface in any description of his life. First of all, he was a *non-judgmental and flexible person*, open to the suggestions of God as he slowly understood them during his two or three years of self-assessment. Secondly, he learned to be *trusting and responsive to others' needs* as a result of the approval he had received from significant persons in his life. Thus he was able to transfer this response easily to God, his heavenly Parent. Finally, because he had enough self-confidence to take risks and tolerate frustration, he was *pledged to a continuing struggle*, not only to achieve heroic virtue in the face of physical and mental anguish, but also to define his own charism and role within his religious foundation. This natural maturity was the substratum of his charism.

The opening paragraphs of this book refer to the "motive force" of faith as awareness of one's perfectibility and the desire to actualize oneself by all the human experiences possible, including the metaphysical and transcendental ones. St. Francis extrapolated his own self-concept to include the whole world. Because the Son of God became the Son of Man, human nature was eminently perfectible and every human being must be respected and unconditionally regarded without prejudice. *This optimism about each person's potential to share in God's nature made him propose the high Gospel ideals* without glossing over them or reducing their force by some rationalization. This is one of the components of the Franciscan charism.

This idealism was, indeed, a part of the romantic personality of St. Francis, as we observed above. The itinerant troubadours of his age inspired him to be he herald of his Great King. And so he composed and sang religious ballads, especially in French, the language of that land where Jesus Christ was so greatly honored in the Blessed Sacrament. The knights of his day, although scarcely above reproach in the motives for battle, were ideally committed to espouse the cause of the poor, the widows, the undefended. And so he identified easily with these champions in his own objectives. It is not unlikely that the saint, were he alive today, would make a little "soul music" on his guitar or identify with astronauts in a wholly different set of metaphors.

What is probably most engaging about he personality of St. Francis was his *freedom of self-expression in religious matters.* This is the obvious consequence of his trust in God to provide inspirations and of trust in man to accept them wholeheartedly. Whoever was willing to "put on Christ" and embrace the Gospel life could certainly be trusted to find his individual way to God. In that sense St. Francis was a sign to his brothers; they were not to imitate him, except in the sense of being free to become what grace had made of them. Not everyone had to leap naked into snow; not everyone could stop a passing Emperor and tell him to behave; not everyone could stand in a meadow and preach to the birds. But all could come to know God and know themselves, and the "truth would set them free."

St. Francis wished to become *transparent to all men.* He could matter of factly predict the phenomenal expansion of his community and his conversations with God about it with no apparent prejudice to his humility—which is another word for realistic self-evaluation. He could openly indulge his poetic fantasies. He liked the lark because she had a gray habit and cowl, like brothers, and was satisfied to find a few seeds along the road in exchange for praising God. He was unafraid to be sentimental and to risk others' doubts about his virility (and possibly sanity) by buying a lamb intended for slaughter, because it reminded him of the Lamb of God. He opened his emotional life to the scrutiny of men by asserting, "I cry over the sufferings of the Lord Jesus Christ. In fact, I should not be embarrassed to traverse the world, crying aloud for him" (*Legend of the Three Companions*). His transparency drove him to be utterly honest about his own spiritual life. We read in the *Second Life* by Celano that he wanted everyone to know that he had eaten food prepared with animal fat when he was sick during Lent. He likewise sewed patches on the outside of his tunic to match the fur he had to wear on the inside to protect him from the cold during his illness. The point is that a Franciscan is not necessarily required to copy what may be alien to his own spiritual growth, but rather to present that same kind of transparency to the world. For example, St. Francis begged food to bring to Cardinal Hugolino's table when the latter invited him to dinner. The prelate found this offensive. His guest replied that bringing food which had been begged in imitation of the poor Christ, who had lived from alms in his public life, was also bringing honor to Hugolino himself. To some of us this might sound a little smug and condescending.

As one discovers the components of the Franciscan charism, such as optimism about man's perfectibility, freedom of religious self-expression, transparency of life, and so forth, one cannot escape comparing the facts of history. In time the Franciscan Order fell into a lockstep kind of structure. Aware that individuality and especially the mobility required for self-expression were inhibited by monastic structures, huge institutions, and ritualized behavior, St. Francis envisioned *small and flexible groups of men*, like the twelve Apostles, who could rapidly respond to people's needs. An important example of St. Francis' liberating expression of religious life was a decreasing stress on the mandatory ascetical practices of other religious institutes, such as fasting, making the recitation of the monastic office more essential than ministerial service, stability of location, and so forth. He was undoubtedly harsh with himself because he apologized to Brother Ass before he died, but he imposed fewer demands than the founders before him. Certain fasts he legislated for the brothers when they were home, but on the road they were to eat what was set before them, as Christ the Lord told the Apostles to do when they were distressed over possible ritual impurities in the preparation of food. Thus St. Francis *related asceticism to charism*; it served the charism. The supreme asceticism was self-denial through self-giving.

All of the components mentioned so far can be applied to many merely natural ventures. Therapists, teachers, statesmen, research scientists, artists, and others must possess freedom of expression, transparency to others affected by their mission, mobility, and optimism. But for a charism to be supernatural, it must have the approval of the believing community. To be "official," the charism must have the *approval of the hierarchy*. As the previous chapter pointed out, St. Francis was not hostile to authority; he did not have to rebel to show that he was different. But he was careful not to seek official sanction of his life style until he was himself assured of its viability.

St. Francis therefore decided to take his band to see Pope Innocent III, who is reputed to have been the strongest personality among the popes of the Middle Ages. It was likely that he was suspicious of any wandering band of men claiming to live the Gospel life, because several groups had already upset the populace in France and the Low Countries by attacking abuses in the Church while they themselves were attempting to live the evangelical life of poverty. St. Francis would not have been unaware of the fracas in the Transalpine Church. "Brothers, I see that the merciful Lord intends to increase our numbers. Let us approach the holy Roman Church, our mother, and make the Pope aware of what the Lord has begun to accomplish by us, in order that we may continue with his good will and directives" (*Legend of the Three Companions*). Thus the liaison with the hierarchy, begun under the aegis of Guido Secondi, Bishop of Assisi, was carried to the Vicar of Christ.

St. Francis at this time was satisfied with verbal approval. We may attribute this attitude to his simplicity and optimism, or to his uncertainty about how long his band would remain together. Because an event of this kind occurred in the dim and hallowed past in a so-called "age of faith," it was not less subject to criticism and doubt, particularly from the participants. To rebuild a few churches is not the same thing as taking seriously the divine mandate to preach the Gospel to every creature. In any case the group was tonsured as a sign of affiliation to the Church and returned to Rivo Torto for two years. This was the first fixed abode of the Order, but it was abandoned when the local herdsmen complained that the friars arrogated a hut long in use by themselves. Subsequently St. Francis made the Chapel of St. Mary of the Angels in the valley, called the Portiuncula, the center of his activities and the abode to which his heart ever turned.

The bishops, however, were standoffish about the patched friars who invaded their bailiwicks. The saint ultimately realized that the transparency of their personal lives was not enough to win over the clergy. After all, his was a lay movement, without professional theologians; there was only one priest, Sylvester, in the original group. Orthodoxy must always be one of the chief concerns ofthe hierarchy. But if the Pope himself granted a bull of approval, the bishops would not feel so uneasy. "Under the Church's supervision," as a reliable biographer of St. Francis puts the words into the saint's mouth, "the holy observance of evangelical purity will continuously flower. She will not allow the fragrance of our life to vanish for a single moment" (Celano, *Second Life)*.

At the beginning of both Rules St. Francis legislates loyalty to the Church. No one may be received contrary to the form and custom of the holy Church. In Chapter Nineteen of the *First Rule* he writes, "All the brothers must be Catholics, and act and speak in the Catholic manner. If anyone should separate from the Catholic faith and way of life in word or in deed and refuse to amend, he shall be expelled from our fraternity." To reinforce the link with the Church he mentions in the *Second Rule* that the brothers are bound to request a Cardinal of the holy Roman Church as governor, protector, and monitor of the Order.

If St. Francis had his way, he would have refused any documents that might have been given him to prevent criticism or persecution of his nascent Order. He consistently warned his brothers against seeking written privileges and censured those who had done so during his absence in the Holy Land. He felt that the word of the Supreme Pontiff sufficed, for example, to be the guarantee for the plenary indulgence of the Portiuncula, which was remarkable for its time. In his *Second Rule*, he is adamant in forbidding the brothers to preach in any diocese where the bishop has not given them leave. "My proposal is to soften the heart of prelates through holy humility and respect. Then their invitation to preach will carry greater weight than documents" (*Mirror of Perfection)*. Nor would the saint accept gifts of land and plan a friary without the same personally granted permission. As a whole, St. Francis was characterized by unswerving reverence for the clergy. He returns to this theme often in his writings. "We have been given to the clergy as helpers for the salvation of souls. The needs that they are unable to satisfy should be supplied by us" (Celano, *Second Life*). It was precisely because they preached the word of God and confected the Body of Christ that they have a title to the reverence of a Franciscan. "The Lord gave and continues to give me trust in priests who live according to the pattern of the holy Roman Church... I refuse to look for sin in them, because I see the Son of God in them, and thus they are my lords" (*Testament*).

Religious are not bound to a particular prelate once they have received papal approval, it is true. They belong to the hierarchy in its totality as focused in the Holy Father. The division of the Church into dioceses is a human administrative decision. Therefore, although a religious institute needs episcopal approval to function locally, the Vatican II documents are clear in prohibiting bishops from controlling the expression of a religious charism (*Christus Dominus* 33, and *Perfectae Caritatis* 8-10). Nevertheless, in the light of St. Francis' own charism, Franciscans of every kind (unlike members of an eremitical order, for example) are to assist the presbyterate of the diocese in their functions, but according to the charism we are attempting to define in these pages. Further, if Franciscans today were to reassess their current position in every diocese and, bypassing all their well-documented privileges, ask the bishop whether they should remain at the posts, change their roles, or surrender the apostolates, they would display the kind of dependence on the good will of the hierarchy that St. Francis considered essential to keep his brothers loyal to the Church. Thus Franciscans would prove their mobility also. They could not allow themselves to become attached to fixed abodes. It is not as if there were other areas of a nation or of the world lacking in which to serve. Perhaps this concept would force religious to "put their best foot forward" at all times. House of formation, recuperation, retirement, and so forth would not be included in the frequent reassessment by ecclesiastical superiors, of course, inasmuch as they do not essentially, but only accidentally, serve a ministerial function in a diocese.

Out of the freedom, mobility, and loyalty to the Church grows another dimension of the Franciscan charism, that is, *secularity*. This is made out to be a pejorative term in some quarters. But its denotation is "involved with the world." In contrast with the major trends among religious institutes prior to St. Francis, he thrust his men into the world's pursuits. In time the friars became papal legates to all parts of the world, even distant Tartary, and bishops and cardinals. Six or seven even rose to the papacy. They were to implement the religious aspect in business, art, government, the military, rural life. This was not to despiritualize the friars' lives. St. Francis preached to the Sultan and his court, noblemen and knights, popes and cardinals, businessmen and farmers. Even more fundamentally, as Pope Benedict XV proclaimed, he made *religious life common property* as a project of his secularity. Tertiaries, who are one time even professed religious vows and wore a distinctive garb, were active in all departments of human endeavor. Because such involvement has been common for centuries of religious life, the innovation of St. Francis is not so apparent to the modern observer.

Monks who lived a life of relative sequestration could not very well present the image of Christ in his full public life, praying in solitude, preaching, training followers to succeed him, laying down his life for others. St. Francis proposed to verify his charism in a *life style as literally close to Christ as possible*. This *emphasis on the humanity of Christ* represented a change in the public and private life of the Church before his time. The joyful glorification of Christ and awareness of his immanence, which was true in the Apostolic Age of the Church in particular, when the memory of the Lord was most vivid, ceded after the time of Constantine to an emphasis on the unapproachable dignity of the God-Man. The awesome majesty of God was implemented by the complex ceremonials surrounding the person of an Oriental emperor of Persia or Byzantium. The action of the Mass was hidden by the iconostasis to remind the worshiper of the gulf between the mystery of God and the lowliness of man.

St. Francis, on the other hand, distilled the joy of living from the Gospels, the Acts, and the Pauline Letters, which continually convey greetings of joy and peace. Our saint's emphasis on the humanness of Christ was coupled with and based upon the Bible. His random opening of the book of the Gospels, the statements of his biographers make clear his reliance on the word of God. Also, for example, there are twelve sentences in Chapter Eleven of the *First Rule*; in them appear fifteen quotations and paraphrases from the Scriptures. "I want my brothers to study the Gospels and progress in truthful knowledge in such a way as to advance at the same time in pure simplicity. Thus they shall not divorce the dove's simplicity from the serpent's wisdom, inasmuch as our good Master joined them in his holy statements" (St. Bonaventure, *Major Legend*).

Lex orandi, lex credendi says the ecclesiastical aphorism: your prayers reflect your beliefs. St. Francis' identification with Christ in his life style brought new theological concepts into doctrinal statements as well as to popular and liturgical prayer forms. We remember how he set up the first creche at Greccio, Italy, at Christmas, his favorite of all feasts. One of the great thrills of his mortal life was to travel to the Holy Land (under the safe conduct of the Sultan, whom he had astounded by his simple faith) and walk the earth sanctified by the feet of our Lord. The sacramental presence of Christ in the Eucharist was central to the prayer life of St. Francis, for it was the nearest a man could get on earth to the total person of Christ. This intimate involvement with his brother, Christ, occasioned the sealing of his flesh with the very wounds borne by Christ. Even if one were to reject the supernatural origin of the stigmata (if it were in the natural order) it might bespeak a more remarkable phenomenon in that St. Francis made this identification by sheer force of his will and the sum of his experiences and reflections, rather than that it was caused by the divine intervention. God is also the master of nature; his grace can just as effectively join man's natural process of symbolization without altering physical laws.

Although this crucifixion was not without its physical pains, as witnesses to his life attested, God answered the petition of the saint to feel Christ's anguish even more fully. The Order he had founded, almost unwillingly, became so complex, needed such administrative acumen, and to such a degree lost individual contact with him on an intimate level, that he was torn by its loss of mobility and the family spirit. Before the Chapter on May 14, 1217, at the Portiuncula, he verbalized his fear that his very naivete and lack of learning might put off the educated brothers who had been received into the Order. Although the contrary occurred on this occasion, the next decade saw the administrative leadership of the community slip from Francis' hands. His own confreres did reject him, save as a figurehead. "Since my brothers recognize what they are to accomplish and what to avoid (without me), there is nothing left for me to do but teach them by my example. That is why I have been given to them during life and after death" (*Mirror of Perfection*). Although the saint excused himself from governing because of ill health, there are the graver reasons that he finally refused to argue with lax brothers and that he saw the community evolving a charismatic pattern that was inspired by his own, yet differing from it.

Ultimately the testimonial to happiness from identifying with the Crucified is the *perfect joy* of St. Francis. The well-known story is not a theoretical proposition of St. Francis; once more he had the knowledge of experience. The source is the prejudicial *Little Flowers*, but the story line is definitely St. Francis. When Brother Leo asked what perfect joy might be for a Franciscan, the saint replied that it was not in the power to cure and raise the dead, as Christ did; not in knowing all things, including the future and men's hearts, as Christ did; not in the ability to convert all men to God, as Christ did. But if they were standing in the freezing rain, hungry and dirty, at the door of the Portiuncula, and the doorkeeper were to deny them entrance, use abusive language, call them thieves in disguise, and beat them with a stick—"and if we bear all this patiently, keeping in mind the sufferings of Christ, who is worthy of all praise, and how much we should bear out of love for him, Brother Leo, then remember, this is perfect joy!" In the life of St. Francis we see no "credibility gap" between his assertions and his experiences.

A final dimension of the personal charism of our saint must be mentioned before a resume of all the qualities can be integrated into a single definition. We see in St. Francis a *predilection for the disadvantaged and suffering.* This was not only a humanitarian service—although it was also that. Although humanity is perfectible, the most optimistic person could see that the poor and lepers, for example, had a greater need of spiritual help precisely because the drudgery of physical survival left little time for reflective prayer and diminished belief that God cared for them. Isaiah the prophet made the proclamation of the Good News to poor people one of the signs of the Messiah's coming. If it is true that every Christian shares in the mystery of Christ on earth, then the disadvantaged share especially in Christ's suffering and abandonment.

As Christ had wealthy and influential friends on earth, Joseph of Arimathea, Nicodemus, Mary, Martha, and Lazarus, St. Francis had his Count Orlando, Giacoma de Settesoli, Cardinal Hugolino, and others. Nevertheless he called his brothers the *minores,* the "unimportant." Alert to the needs of the poor, however, St. Francis forbade his brothers to beg at the "table of the Lord" (contrary to popular opinion), unless the labor of their own hands failed to support them. Thus they were not to be parasites in society, but, like St. Paul, join their crafts to their apostolate. Nor would the indigent be deprived of success in their begging. *Poverty* is a consequesce of assuming the apostolic life and is a practical demand of preaching to the poor without a "credibility gap." In Chapter Nine of the *First Rule*, St. Francis exhorts the brothers to converse with lowly and despised persons, with the poor and weak, with the sick and lepers, and with beggars in the streets. They were to beg alms as a way of assuming the life of Christ, his mother, and the Apostles.

In summary, we see the personality of a man who grew up into a responsive, flexible, self-confident person, able to take risks. This was the *man* Francis. He had a spiritually based optimism about man's potential to become God's son. His freedom in expressing himself in religious matters was coupled with a willingness to be transparent to others in the process. He attempted to copy the visible ministry of Christ and his Apostles, a leader of a small, mobile band of men, with lives uncluttered by bureaucracy and a multiplicity of regulations. Asceticism was not assumed for its own sake, but only as a consequence of the apostolate and as an imitation of what Christ did. His loyalty to the institutional Church was complete; his adherence to its doctrines was unswerving. But he had no desire to stand outside the pale of the profane world; for him the world was naturally sacred, and the secular and sacred worlds had to become coterminous. Thus, while he assumed a life style as utterly like Christ's as possible, he tried to extend what was originally a lay movement to include even married persons and those unable to copy the itinerant way of Jesus. Whatever deepened his likeness to the human Christ, including physical and mental anguish, contributed to his perfect joy. His mission as an "unimportant brother" of men was especially to the disadvantaged and the poor. This was the *saint and founder*, Francis.

All these factors can now be examined for their common denominator. Life style and spiritually based personality can be fused into a single charismatic concept. Only then what is the enduring legacy to his religious institute can be interpreted existentially according to the common experiences of its members. As the founder expressed it, "O Lord, in this final era of the world, mindful of your ancient loving-kindness, you have established this Order of brothers to give stability to your faith and to perfect the mystery of the Gospel through them" (Celano, *Second Life*).

"To perfect the mystery of the Gospel through this new Order of brothers": this process is both grandiose and obscure for want of written texts. Biographers have managed to put the pieces together by combining legends, myths, and scraps of writings about or by the founder. Between the seventeeth-century Luke Wadding (1623) and the twentieth-century Lemmens (1904), there was no critical edition of St. Francis' writings in order to discern his creative expression of religious life. Luke Wadding mentions over 200 "authentic" writings by the founder, but Fr. Cajetan Esser in our century accepts about 35, including eight he dictated.

When Francis went off to Spoleto to take up war he had his own *propositum,* or vision or personal objective, but when he returned and began to pray before the Crucifix of San Damiano, he began to pray for the Lord's *mandatum,* or commision for divine agenda. In other words, "God help me to surrender my own *propositum,* so I can fill your *mandatum.*" This is the essence of the Prayer before a Crucifix. Francis used to jot down his prayers and teach them to the friars, as "We adore you, O Christ, and we bless you, because by your holy cross you have redeemed the world." (This tradition began with St. Anselm of Canterbury.)

Although the early biographies tell of his usually precipitous conversions, we are more interested in the struggle preceding conversion. One group of scholars did not think his writings very significant anyway for a systematic theology of "Franciscanism" until St. Bonaventure. The *Primitive Rule* was lost; it was simply a handful of sayings from the New Testament which the first friars memorized. These were favorite quotations of St. Francis; they probably included such exhortations as: "Take nothing for the journey"; "If you wish to be my disciple, go, sell what you have and give it to the poor, take up your cross daily and come, follow me."

The *Rule of 1221* (without a papal bull to support it) was considerably diffuse and weighed down with long Scripture texts. Inasmuch as the uneducated friars could not read and generally had to memorize the text, St. Francis was asked to shorten the Rule, which was finally presented to the Pope. This was the *Rule of 1223*, (with a papal bull to confirm it). This is the Rule observed by the First Order priests and brothers today. Of course, one cannot forget the *Testament* Francis wrote, which is like a retrospective of his spiritual life and career. It is the most touching and revealing of all his writings. It was not a supplement to the Rule, although some friars treated it that way; it was rather a memorial and an exhortation, or a *fervorino*. Francis had written an earlier *Testament* from Siena when he thought he was dying, but there is just a fragment remaining.

The world of St. Francis was unified, but remained a hierarchical system both in Church and State. Whereas today our unity seems to derive from a homogeneous mass of citizens observed horizontally. But in the Middle Ages the citizens looked up or down, that is, vertically at their society. Under the metaphor of domestic animals the clergy were the *sheep*, the warriors were the *dogs*, and the peasantry were the *oxen*. *Orantes, bellatores*, and *laboratores*. Even the religious Orders made distinctions, but St. Francis tried to divest his Order of classes and rank. Having begun a lay movement, he accpeted one and all without worrying about class distinctions. Strangely, he did defer to those with education on some occasions and asked a brother from the upper social class to be their spokesman to Church authority, as in the case of Bernard of the First Companions when they approched the pope.

He preferred to serve the Church without books or lectures to prepare preachers, which ended by not working very well. In this case poverty interfered with evangelization. Francis did not want so large an Order that he could not personally influence, even though he felt the Church would protect his ideals. Yet the Founder did not criticize society nor the Church. Perhaps that was his secret as a "man of peace." He did make himself out to be a "righter of wrongs" or the "champion of the afflicted." He formed no committees and did not present himself as arbitrator. But when the citizens of a town saw he was indifferent to money, power, and clout, they forgot their empty quarrels and were ready to forgive. He tried not to take sides, even against the Gubbio people-eater wolf.

Thus the Founder made his contemporaries uncomfortable and even embarrassed about their power and privilege. His life was an implied criticism, not of possessions, but of greed and comfort. Naked we came into the world and naked shall we leave it. We cannot buy admission into the Kingdom of God.

St. Francis saw the Church waiting at every turn of the road to mark him as her own. The Church gave him the sacramental strength and later the programs. One can ship out on the vessel of Peter as a stowaway or a hired hand, an indenture or a pirate or a volunteer. St. Francis came aboard as the most willing of deckhands. At the same time he felt utterly free, yet completely submissive and chained. You have to possess your life to give it away. You have to give it away in order to keep it. You cannot surrender what is not yours.

Surrender was something about which St. Francis knew a lot. When the time arrived for his passing (which Franciscans translate as *"transitus"*) we rightly ask what the Founder was celebrating. His final eighteen months offered small reasons. He saw divisions within his Order; to some minds he himself was the focus of the division. The second

generation of friars accepted some conveniences, even lax-
ities. Francis' health was at its lowest ebb. He was tempted
regarding his salvation, that his actions had been in vain. Even
the devils, it is written, mocked him for treating Brother Ass
too hard. He seemed more than ever an exile, a wanderer. At
the command of Hugolino in the summer of 1225, he went to
see the papal physician in Rieti, near Assisi. He was so weak
that he spent seven weeks at San Damiano, where he had once
began and where he composed most of the Canticle of the
Creatures. (The location of the Canticle has also been given
as the Portiuncula and Fonte Colombo whither next he traveled.) At Fonte Columbo he was subjected to the strange
medieval therapies of blood-letting and having his temples
cauterized by hot irons on the theory it would improve his
eyesight. The poor saint later died of "doctoring."

That last winter he wrote or dictated his last two circu-
lar letters, including the one to the *General Chapter* of 1226
regarding reverence for the Eucharist. Then he was sent off
to Siena for more pain and more medical interventions. He
was no longer his own man. Blind, enduring pounding headaches, his stomach eaten away, probably by cancer, burning
up with recurrent quartan fever, suffering the pains of the
stigmata—what else did he have to surrender?

His dear friend who had captained the skirmish long
ago in Assisi when Francis was captured, who was the saint's
vicar and protector and friend, Brother Elias, later much ma-
ligned, came to fetch the dying man and take him home to
Assisi. An armed guard from Assisi joined Elias, for fear that
another town might claim the saint's body if he died within
their jurisdiction. One record shows he was taken to the
bishop's "palace" in Assisi, within the walls for safekeeping;
other accounts disagree.

He shared his final intimte thoughts with his brothers,
especially Brother Elias, on whom he placed his hands, in order to bless all the Order through Elias. Anxious to reinforce
his charism and meaning in the world, he completed his *Tes-*

tament. When a doctor from Arezzo told him he would soon die of dropsy, which today we call "congestive heart failure," he wrote the final lines of the Canticle, "Be praised, my Lord, for Sister Death, from whose embrace no man can escape."

Again with men-at-arms Brother Elias took Francis to Portiuncula where he loved best to be. He paused to turn his face toward Assisi and bless his hometown with a blessing recorded for the ages, "May it ever be the dwelling of those who glorify your blessed name!"

Consciously fulfilling his charism to the end, he asked to be stripped naked on the ground as Jesus had died on the cross. The local guardian had to "lend" him a habit for the sake of decency. He sent messages to Clare and Jacopa who was already en route. On October 2 he remembered the Last Supper and blessed and broke and shared bread with the friars. On October 3, his last day on earth, he had the Passion according to St. John read to him and he wept for love of his Lord. Thus, after reciting Psalm 141, he passed into history and the Kingdom of God.

This was only the 46th year of his life and the 20th of his full conversion to Christ. At dawn on Sunday, October 4, his body was taken to San Giorgio in Assisi (later to be named Santa Chiara) for temporary interment. The cortege passed under the windows of San Damiano, so his sisters, the Poor Clares, might look upon him for the last time.

Did the Founder celebrate something on the evening of October 3, 1226? In imitation of the Master, he said *yes* to Sister Death, his guide and gate to eternity. She was his down payment on resurrection. The Church was his mother, Lady Poverty his bride, Sister Death his joy. Hers is the touchstone that transforms our leaden lives into golden triumphs of the Kingdom. Hers is the measuring stick that gauges this earth by the eternal world-to-come. She took his hand as a friend does, assuring him he would live tomorrow and tomorrow in God and through his brothers and sisters.

CHAPTER VI

The Franciscan Charism Defined

As Jesus spoke to us in the words of the Bible, so St. Francis highlights his charism and ministry through his writings, although there are few extant and many spurious. I already mentioned that his first *Primitive Rule* was largely a collection of the Founder's favorite Bible passages. In fact, to discern most religious founder's charisms, the first point of research is precisely the favorite Scriptural texts. Especially by comparison with he two later expanded Rules, we can easily surmise that the "missionary" exhortation lay at the heart of the Franciscan enterprise: Take nothing for your journey, not a second tunic nor a staff or wallet. But depend on the generosity of those to whom you minister, and eat whatever is set before you. If they don't heed your preaching, shake the dust from your sandals as a testimony that the townspeople have not become part of the "Holy Land."

Factually the life style of the first friars was like the living conditions adopted by the heretic contemporaries of St. Francis. Yet the saint was interiorly urged by his convictions to demonstrate the Gospel inspiration to the Holy Father, and that they were bonafide Catholics.

The so-called *First Rule of 1221*, never confirmed by a papal document, has been viewed by scholars too much in terms of its legalities, as annual chapters, formation, major superiors, and particularly wandering "outside obedience," that is, outside the jurisdiction or province or region to which they properly belonged. In contrast to these free-wheeling members, some friars were being seduced by a monasticizing influence. Neither attitude conformed to the Gospel. But a reading of the *Rule of 1221* shows how weighted the document is with Bible texts. Once more Francis is indicating that his growing family is to live according to the form of the Gospel. Therein lies the charism of the Founder, but it must be further specified. Moreover, this charism must apply to the Clares and the Third Order.

The *Second Rule of 1223*, is confirmed by a papal document, *Solet annuere*. This is Francis' mature spirit at work; he uses mostly hortatory subjunctive verbs so as not to command so much as to persuade. Students of the Franciscan charism keep groping for the essential charism in the *Second Rule* and call it work, prayer, obedience, minority, fraternity, the apostolic life, a complex of relationships, poverty, service to others, "itinerance," etc. By this time the Founder had distanced himself from the administration of the Order and a more literate author (than Francis' rudimentary Latin) wrote down the thoughts of the Founder.

For those who sought a temporary respite from the active life, St. Francis provided a short and simple *Rule for Hermitages*, such as he himself undertook often in life. But even the life of communal solitude (to consist of four friars) had to demonstrate Gospel values and the common life. This will have to be verified about the Clares and Secular Franciscans, too.

A final word about the *Testament*, which introduces new "essential" features into the Franciscan charism, such as being totally Catholic. St. Francis strongly pointed out that he was led by divine inspiration, not copying other earlier Churchmen, to live according to the form of the holy Gospel. Always there was a suggestion of risk, without being protected by papal and episcopal documents, that outsiders would reject them, bishops would refuse them access to their jurisdictions, and the laity abandon them. Sociologists tell us that our "role opposites" help determine our meaning and function, hence those hostile to the Franciscan movement, indeed, helped to determine how he Order would prosper or fail.

Other writings of St. Francis cannot be overlooked, and the Order is enriched by the opinions of Fr. Kajetan Esser, whose works have not yet endured the test of time, but are very influential. Meanwhile there are so many controversies regarding Thomas of Celano's two *Lives* and the *Treatise on Miracles* and their sources, followed by the painful issue of Brother Elias' excommunication for siding with the Holy Roman Emperor Frederick II, then finally the work of St. Bonaventure in editing the Order's official biography, that the matter of which book is most useful and true is best left for scholars to decide and decipher. I do not find them useful for delineating the Franciscan charism. In any case the *General Chapter* of Paris in 1266 did away with both of Celano's *Lives*, and Bonaventure's *Legends* survived. Naturally this was grist for the mills of two pseudo-biographers, Anthony Mockler (*Francis of Assisi: The Wandering Years*) and Adolf Holl (*The Last Christian*), both of whom had hefty battle-axes to grind and wished to preserve their own inane views of the Founder. It is obvious that these two "authors" are antinomian and anti-Establishment and felt arrogantly superior by making Francis anti-Catholic! Thus shallow and silly men are vaguely amusing as they try to stand against the universal opinion of thousands of friars, laypersons, and historians. Holl even quotes Paul Sabatier as saying the *Testament* was tantamount to a revocation of the *Second Rule.* The instincts of the many are to be preferred to the vagaries of the fringe.

If the Franciscan charism seems so vague, we can adduce several reasons for it. Our charism is not linked to a particular apostolate: our Order is more "representational" than "functional." We are geared to "becoming" more than to "producing." When the "process" of ministry overrides the "person" who is ministering, then our charism becomes less credible. These distinctions are more or less true of all religious, of course. But the distinctions must be kept in mind, because St. Francis, unlike most leaders of men in history, did not dwarf his followers by his overwhelming presence. He helped them to grow taller by his creative approach to religious life. Hence the Franciscan charism tends to assume the face of the one who possesses it. (And Franciscans like to think that, even when historical events calcified the life style of the Order, they remained uncategorized as individuals, thanks to the liberating spirit of St. Francis.)

There are several other reasons why the Franciscan charism appears so nebulous. There are so many species and subdivisions of Franciscanism, particularly among the sisterhoods, that they tend to obscure the general pattern in which we should commonly live. Also, many founders after St. Francis incorporated into their movements some of the innovations mentioned in the previous chapter; thus the special Franciscan character of the innovations was lost. Then again, even within the same branch of the Order, individual provinces, because of their unique development or apostolate, put a special cast on our common charism as their particular spirit. But the national origin of a province and its orientation to missions or teaching or parochial work need not submerge the basic Franciscan self-concept. A final point concerning the indecision with which we view our own corporate personality is that there is just one spirituality—putting on Christ, who called himself the way, the truth, and our life. All charisms are to be subsumed under the basic Christian struggle to make Christ present to the Church and to the world.

Perhaps the main obstacle to defining the Franciscan charism in the past was that it was narrowly confined to the First Order, rather than to what St. Francis was attempting to accomplish within the whole Church. The definition must apply to both sexes and include the lay tertiaries. Thus we propose here that *the Franciscan charism is to demonstrate that the life of preaching and service led by Christ, his apostles, and the disciples in first-century Palestine can be successfully lived, even in its externals, in any century and locale.* "Preaching" is not to be understood in the narrow, formal sense, and "service" is broader than the active life. Every phrase in the definition, including the distinction made between apostles and disciples, has significance. Another way to express the Franciscan charism more succinctly is that *it is our mandate to recall men and women to the Apostolic Age of the Church.* After St. Francis left the scene of his work upon his death, he still lingered on by the force of his personality. It goes without saying, of course, that it was the Holy Spirit who guided the first disciples of St. Francis. The existence of opposing ideas among equally sincere followers of Francis in succeeding centuries is another instance of the polarization mentioned earlier in this book.

The Franciscan Order, we then see, is in its threefold dimension to replicate the experiences of the apostles, who in turn consecrated other men for the task of establishing communities of Christians. In these earliest communities we read also of the holy women dedicated to the service of the faithful and of the world at large. We can find further analogies, such as that between secular tertiaries and those first apostolic foundations which were most responsive to the teaching of Christ, even to the point of "sharing everything in common" (cf. Acts 2:44). This recall to the Apostolic Age is our "theological model" or the framework of our ministerial labor. Here once more "ministry" refers both to the lay and to the priestly state, and to both men and women. The prophetic role of St. Francis was precisely to give voice to this earlier variety of expression in religion, the former mobility of mission, the concern of primitive Christians to rise from the Eucharistic agape and serve the disadvantaged, and their joyful involvement with the secular world. Above all, St. Francis gave voice and meaning to the vivid memory of the human Christ as if he had ascended into heaven just yesterday. As Pope Benedict XV remarked, "St. Francis made religious life common property." This quotation can be restated that evangelical poverty, chastity, and obedience are possible to priest, brother, sister, married or unmarried lay person.

Every component of the Franciscan charism must be related to the individual's perception of himself somehow serving—"I am in your midst as the one who serves you"—and somehow preaching—"faith comes through hearing." The question arises why St. Francis, who is supposed to be a kind of guidepost or novicemaster even today, was so adamant in enforcing certain Gospel insights. A guidepost, of course, has to convey its meaning adequately. Hence, as was said above, after our saint returned from the Holy Land to Italy in the spring of 1220 or 1221, he repudiated such changes in his charism as large and permanent establishments, monastic observances, and difficult fasts inconsistent with alms gathering and traveling. He was especially unhappy with written privileges that led to pretentiousness and induced a certain laxity, because the brothers were under less constraint to give the more important documentation of their lives well lived. The brothers should not have whereon to lay their heads, he said. Fasting was the privilege of imitating Christ in his forty-day abnegation, but should not become a regulation for its own sake. Therefore every aspect of the brothers' lives began by a comparison with the statement of Scriptures. We hear St. Francis say (in words whose viewpoint was later echoed by St. Vincent de Paul addressing the Daughters of Charity): "Wherever we move, we keep our cell with us. Brother Body is our cell. The hermit who dwells inside is our soul, keeping contact with God and meditating upon him. In fact, if the soul does not stay at home in reflection, any cell made by hands is useless for a religious" (*Mirror of Perfection*).

Because charism is subject to hierarchy, if it is to achieve an "official" status, religious need formal and precise instruction in the charism. This is to be given within an ideal community. A house of formation is the place where the person spontaneously discovers how he or she can be set free to love others, meanwhile "practicing" this concept and testing it under the supervision of persons well suited to provide these experiences. But even in houses of training, the life style must include *service* to others inside and outside the immediate community and *preaching*, not just by example, but also by "exhorting one another" and "confessing their sins to one another," and by "joyful songs and spiritual canticles," as we read of the primitive Church in the New Testament. The community must be small enough for a continual face-to-face charity with every other member. Thus each member learns to become transparent to the rest; no one should be able to "escape" into anonymity and facelessness.

Each community of Franciscans should follow the theological model of the apostles and the disciples. The disciples were those persons who were not mobile, but stayed at home as part of the local community formed by a spiritual leader. Like today's secular tertiaries, they had family commitments or were simply unequal to the active life. On the other hand, modern active religious and priests look to the apostles, who shared the experiences of close living, were sent into specific locales to bring the good news, and then returned to be strengthened in conviction and take consolation from their loving community. St. Francis represents the attempt to restore these ideas to the world. If our own time does see a rebirth of this creative expression of religious life, we will immediately have to resist calcification and permanent structuring, of course. To keep the charism alive in the Church, the authority should dismiss a candidate who does not give ample promise of preaching and serving and living in a community of lovers. Incidentally, the small, experimental communities we see rising all over the Catholic world seem to be a recovery of some of the ideas brought out in these pages to explain the Franciscan charism. But if the experiment is merely humanitarian social service, or if the members do not regularly pray, eat, and relax together, then the life style of Christ with the apostles (or the apostles with their constituents) is not convalidated.

Truthfully, it was easier for St. Francis to imitate the life style of the first century during the thirteenth century than it is for us. There is a greater likeness between the first and thirteenth centuries than between our lives and those of just one hundred years ago—in food eaten, fabrics worn, the recreation possible, the careers available, the science known, the philosophy taught. Life for the earlier centuries was geared to the flocks and to the soil, with some merchandising in the larger towns and seaports. Nowadays swift travel, communications media, and technological aids have expanded not only the means of spreading the good news, but also of spreading its competition. It is not so clear in our day what is useful, but not luxurious, what is supportive of nature, but not indulgence. Since Christ or Francis could not have established a precedent, modern Franciscans have to solve the problem—and generally it will be on the individual rather than on the collective level, as is fitting in an Order where individual expression is valued. (The role of the superior will be to keep the aspiration level high.) The existing and past Rules of tertiaries forbade them vanity in dress, for example. Now a lay woman must decide what clothes are vanity for a tertiary, and a religious sister what hair style (for the unveiled) shows preoccupation, as St. Paul warned!

An example of how a charism continues to evolve in its details according to the perceptions of its members and even of its founder can be seen in some passages of the Rule of the First Order. St. Francis seems to be more severe than the Gospel itself, but certainly not holier than Christ. He forbids his brothers to receive coins or money for their labor, allowing only food or goods for their needs. Yet Christ had a treasurer and paid the coin of the tribute; obviously he accepted money. It was only for their missionary journeys, as we read in the sixth chapter of St. Mark (vv. 7 ff.) and in similar passages, that Christ gave a prohibition against receiving coins, for reasons we shall explain. In this chapter of St. Mark we see how Christ toured the villages of Galilee, then sent his Apostles in pairs as a follow-up. They were allowed a staff, but no food, money, or "suitcase." They could have sandals, but not extra tunics. They were to stay in the same house, once they were established in a locality, lest they appear to be unstable or seeking the best accommodations. St. Luke and St. Matthew record Christ as allowing no staff; the point is trivial, but the sense is apparent: simplicity and detachment. The historical point is that Christ did not want his apostles' public image to be less than that of the itinerant rabbis of the day, who lived by donations and the overnight hospitality of the local people. The Apostles probably left their gear with Christ, to whom they had to return to make their report. In any case, one must recover the sense of Scriptures rather than slavishly imitate the externals of St. Francis' life. Every Franciscan must continue to read the Gospels, Acts, and Epistles to garner insights about life style. Historical criticism and comparative literature teach us more precisely about the meaning of the Scriptures on which we found our lives— just as the behavioral sciences help us to achieve personhood.

Later in the passage cited from St. Mark, after the missions of the Apostles were completed, Christ tells them to repair to a secluded place and refresh themselves, just as, members of a religious institute theoretically return to a place of relaxation and mutual love after their daily exertions. Yet when the people discovered what they were going to do, Christ relented and began to teach again, because the people were "like untended sheep" (verse 34). Accessibility to the needy or apostolic availability is the touchstone of the Franciscan life, turning daily chores in an office, kitchen, classroom, or pulpit into an occasion of preaching and serving. In that same passage from St. Mark, Christ is seen feeding the multitude miraculously in promise of the Eucharist. We see him continuously supplying both the temporal and spiritual needs of those "untended sheep."

We see the same accessibility or availability in the life of the early Franciscans. Even when St. Francis retired from superiorship and was debilitated in health, he said, "I believe it pleases God more for me to interrupt my retirement and pursue my labors" (St. Bonaventure, *Major Legend*). As Christ and the Apostles were preaching primarily to possessors of the true revelation of God, the Jews, with a few forays among the Samaritans and the Gentiles of the Decapolis, so St. Francis and his first followers were sent primarily to believers. Yet he was he first religious founder who included a chapter in his Rule about missions to the Saracens and other non-believers. We perhaps can say that St. Francis was attempting to establish ideal communities of lovers at every level of society, priestly, religious and lay. He hoped to convert bishops and priests to the fullness of evangelical life as Christ hoped to convert the Scribes, Pharisees, and Sanhedrin to the fullness of the divine revelation. In the first, thirteenth, or twenty-first century, adults brought up in the true faith are not necessarily ready and committed to living it when the crisis of change is presented to them.

Apparently, in the mind of St. Francis the apostolic life

(which is a narrower concept than the "Gospel life," if we examine the terms) did not necessarily or even typically include formal, pulpit preaching, but rather manual labor, good example, and simple exhortation. "The minister should not grant permission to preach to everyone indiscriminately. In any case, all the brothers should preach by their works" (*First Rule*, Chapter Seventeen). St. Francis has St. Paul, the tentmaker, in mind. He tells the brothers to support themselves by manual labor, not in authoritative positions as chamberlains, cellarers, and overseers; they are to remain inferior to all in the household. Although the Founder makes the canonical distinction of his brothers into "clerics" and "laics" in Chapter Seventeen, as well as in the *Second Rule* and *Testament*, in Chapter Twenty-One of the First Rule he permits all the brothers to give words of exhortation to men and praise to God—of which he immediately subjoins an example. Because of Chapter Nine of the *Second Rule* legislating about the examination and approval of preachers, we can infer that this is once more a reference to pulpit preaching by a priest trained in theology—or at least a "cleric," that is, a deacon, as St. Francis was himself.

We are astonished to read that, by the time of the sixth general, St. Bonaventure, it was forbidden to receive brothers into the Order to be used as domestics in the household, unless the minister general himself allowed it. It was not merely a question of appearing to have servants. St. Bonaventure wished to maintain the status of a clerical order, trained in theology, so the heretical element of some uneducated brothers, which plagued him during his whole generalate, might not rise again. Thus the idea of St. Francis that the unlearned "lay" member of his Order could preach by simple exhortation was lost as part of the charismatic expression of the primitive age of the Friars Minor. There can be no doubt that such preaching can be made by sisters, and by men and women tertiaries within the context of their daily business—that is, if they have the courage to join words to the preaching of good example and service. Truly the teaching of Christian doctrine, which does require training, of course, is a marvelous opportunity to give the exhortation which is so Franciscan. At least "secular" tertiaries at their meetings and "regular" tertiaries (religious brothers and sisters) should deliver public words of exhortation to one another as a matter of course.

Preaching and service, anywhere, anytime, by anyone is proper according to the Gospel. The *First Rule* reads, "Let us hold (fast to) his life and teaching and his holy Gospel." The *Second Rule* continues in the same vein, "The rule and life of the Friars Minor is this, namely, to observe the holy Gospel of our Lord, Jesus Christ." In his *Testament* Francis reinforces this further, "No one showed me what I ought to do, but the Most High himself revealed to me that I ought to live according to the form of the holy Gospel." This must clarify the Franciscan charism, as the beginning sentence of the paragraph specifies the operation.

In his *Letter to the Colossians* (3:1-17) St. Paul encapsulates the consequence of following this Gospel charism. "Set your heart on what pertains to higher realms where Christ is seated at God's right hand. Be intent on things above rather than on things of earth. After all, you have *died*. Your life is now hidden with Christ in God.... What you have done is put aside your old self with its past deeds and put on a new man, one who grows in knowledge as he is formed anew." We who follow the Gospel *die*, that is, get incorporated into the divine projects where our lives remain hidden and Jesus emerges through us. Our "hiddenness" is not meant to be the way of living in the world, but rather the way we are called to live in the Kingdom while we yet live on earth. Actually, the Franciscan charism does not like to distinguish between this earth and the Kingdom. Franciscans try to make these concepts co-extensive. After all, "the Kingdom of God is within you."

We who have died to self did not learn to die suddenly, but by degrees, just as St. Francis died through his career failures. So often, when the world seems to grow cold, God sends some saints to inflame our hearts with Gospel values: simplicity, poverty, humility, joy, charity. Such a person was Francis of Assisi. He was not a theologian, a writer, a pope, but a down-to-earth lover of God and man. To recapitulate, history remembers St. Francis for his 1) creative analysis of religious life, going forth to meet and dialogue with others, instead of staying at home in monasteries. We emphasize his 2) great loyalty to the pope when heresies were rife. We recall his 3) preference for the poor and disadvantaged as lepers and beggars. He 4) loved the humanness of Christ and his weakness, from the Christmas Crib at Greccio to weeping over the passion of Jesus until he became a living crucifix at La Verna.

Now all these (except, obviously, reverence for the pope) emerged in the Gospel life of the Savior. But we can transfer our attention to four insights that correspond to his charism in the Church in a special way. 1) St. Francis had a sense of his creatureliness and imperfection, whereby all believers must hustle for the Kingdom. He was "kin" to every bird and animal and creepy crawly underfoot. Small wonder he composed the "Canticle of Brother Sun." 2) St. Francis was upbeat and optimistic with a knight's chivalry and a crusader's daring, so he took risks gladly. Despite his personal sense of unworthiness and imperfection, his optimism made him believe in the perfectibility of mankind, whereby he expected the highest and best of them. 3) St. Francis was not pretentious, did not pose as a mystic, but was down-to-earth, transparent to all, so "what you see is what you get!" 4) St. Francis teaches us to value people over things and make room and time for them. He didn't wait for people to become lovable, forgivable, and beautiful. That is what Jesus said and did, and the Founder was a "rememberer" of the words and acts of the Lord, who said in a generic way, "Do this in memory of me," going beyond the Eucharist.

We discover this ambivalent attitude recorded in *I Celano*, which describes the saint's frame of mind toward the end of his life. "He did not consider that he had laid hold of his goal as yet, and persevering in his purpose of attaining holy newness of life, he hoped always to make a beginning" (*I Celano*, 103).... "He had been brought to the fullness of grace before God.... nevertheless he thought always to begin more perfect works.... Therefore, he was afire with a very great desire to return to the first beginning of humility, and though he found it necessary to moderate his early rigor because of his infirmity, he would still say: 'Let us begin, brothers, to serve the Lord, for up to now we have made little or no progress.'" In fact, he had a thought to return to the care of lepers and to retire to the most remote places as he once did (*Loc. cit..*)

St. Francis, if we read the above carefully and sympathetically, was often depressed, at least disappointed, then at other times was frenetic with activity. He fought with his family; failed at half a dozen careers; took off all his clothes in public; feared contact with women, even holy women; his adolescent fantasies about the military were unreal; he was rather anti-intellectual; he talked to animals and birds; he had outrageous expectations of others. Why, no vocation director in the world would have accepted him! Then we must ask why we approve and cherish his charism, which must apply to all three Orders with equal correctness and relevance. Everyone who accepts his charism must ask how St. Francis is mediated to him or her personally?

St. Francis recognized and understood God as the Lord of history, all history, even natural history—not only the Lord of Catholics or just of a chosen race, but of all the phenomena of nature that he called "brother" and "sister," coming out of the womb of "mother earth." St. Francis through his universal charism celebrated friendship with all classes, even Sister Death. He celebrated poverty as a Lady to be won. Suffering he celebrated as "perfect joy."

One must ask: how do we use the charism to celebrate the God of the 21st century? Of Brother Skyscraper and Sister Microchip? Of rockets, neon signs and computer programs? If we do not "baptize" politics and science and business, this passing world will continue to claim them. In our post-Christian world whatever we do not celebrate *in* God and *for* God we finally lose to the Kingdom of Man.

St. Francis was a *celebrator* with a worldwide liturgy.

He was a *traveler*, always on the move looking for his dream-fulfillment, a changed world.

He was a *tip-toe person*, poised always to look with silent awe at creation and then a little farther to its Maker.

He was a *rememberer* of what Jesus said and did.

He was a *fringe person* on earth by rejecting its values and preferring the marginated poor, outcasts and lepers.

St. Francis was a *thresholder* in heaven's antechamber, waiting for the promise of eternal life—to which may God lead us all.

CHAPTER VII

The Common Life and Individuation

To belong to a community of worshipers is part of the Christian life. The "common life," as the phrase is used here, refers to the familial arrangements of most religious *institutes*. But the religious *state*, as it was defined in preceding chapters, does not require the common life by its nature—although throughout history that is how most institutes evolved. In the light of the broad definition of the Franciscan charism given above, we recall that in both the age of the Apostles and the age of St. Francis the common life in some sense was typical.

Some groups of the early Christians "shared everything in common" (Acts 2:44). They were pledged to show charity above all "to the household of the faith" (Gal. 6:10). The secular tertiary groups analogously are to have a common fund, common prayer life, and an apostolate peculiar to each fraternity, shared in by all. At one time the intensification of baptismal vows included the pronouncing of religious vows by tertiaries living with their families outside the cloister. They even wore distinctive garb prescribed by their laws. As "secular" tertiaries they were completely involved in the world. To underscore their family orientation, St. Francis originally called them the Brothers and Sisters of Penance. As these remarks are implemented in the chapter on Franciscan "secularity," we can confine ourselves here to discussion of "regular" Franciscans of the Three Orders.

St. Francis rejected the earlier forms of religious community. St. Augustine's community of priests was a professional group, tied, as it were, to the ministry of the altar. St. Benedict gave individual monasteries much freedom and autonomy to adapt locally, but to Francis they were too large, stationary, and seemingly only parallel to the world, rather than involved in it. Missionary monks were more to the taste of St. Francis, but they, too, desired mostly to reduplicate their monastic life in another land. The Cluniac reform was based on the kind of community exemption from bishops eschewed by St. Francis, and was geared to the clerical and scholarly life. St. Robert of Molesme, who founded Citeaux, introduced more poverty and made of his foundation a lay movement; but once more St. Francis was not drawn to the large numbers and isolation. In short, our saint wanted smaller, mobile groups, who were loosely attached to a base of operations.

The life of the Apostles was loosely structured. Their "home" was any "base of operations" that was a haven of spiritual fellowship and physical refreshment—a springboard back into full engagement with the world. Regarding the First Order, the very word "friar" means "brother." St. Francis envisioned such families as the pattern of his foundation. The superior was to be the first among equals. "I want my brothers to consider themselves the sons of the same mother," he said. "If anyone requires a tunic, a cord, or anything else, another brother should give it to him gladly.... Indeed, he should practically force him to take it" (Celano, *Second Life*). In both of his Rules, St. Francis goes beyond brotherhood and tells his followers to make known their needs to one another, cherishing each other as a mother might provide for a child. They are even to wash each other's feet (*First Rule*, Chapter Six). When the natural mother of a certain brother was in need, St. Francis sold a copy of the Scriptures to help "our mother," because he felt a special relationship to her through his confrere.

Religious institutes, however they may structure themselves—a community of hermits, monks, friars, secular tertiaries, cloistered nuns, or active sisters—are meant to be a mode, the "city on a hill," to which the Church and the world can look for an example of love and productive cooperation. More than the blood-related family, a religious family has members who are resource persons to each other on an equal footing. Subordination is not be based on the factor of age, but on the greater need to be directed by a person of greater skill—in liturgy, spiritual growth, professional competence, the community's goals as a group. One supposes that the religious family has a greater compatibility because of the members' common objectives and life style, plus the accumulated ongoing experience of many generations.

There are obvious spiritual advantages in living the common life. It provides a check on whether one is acting merely to satisfy one's own ego needs through some "private" apostolate, or is sincerely serving the needs of the Church. Moreover, a worthwhile venture would cease in the event of the originator's death or poor health, or on account of the lack of helpers, unless there is a community to support the project. A member of an institute with a ministry achieved by the common life (unlike most "free-lance" religious) can make his full-time witness explicit. The "isolate" religious must be occupied in making a living, to which the free service of others must be subordinated. The religious identifiable as members of an institute (a special "habit" is not crucial here) should be able to manifest more clearly the glory of the eschatological Church, a community perfected in love. Such persons are, finally, granted access to many more places and persons than are denied them by reason of their obvious institutional membership.

It seems evident that one could carry the notion of a friary or convent as a family too far with respect to parental authority. For Franciscans the local community is like a *family* insofar as it shares a common home and table. The attitude of commonality this engenders does not alter the fact that members of a family have diverse careers and personal fulfillments that can carry them far from their home most of the day. In the religious family, too, a variety of personal endeavors does not necessarily destroy the family attitude.

Further, the local community is like a *brotherhood* insofar as authority arises from within itself, not paternalistically. Although the Order began with a patriarchal government, even in the founder's lifetime it passed to a senatorial, partly representative type of rule. The word "brotherhood" likewise suggests a relationship qualified by a common spiritual ancestry and a corporate destiny.

Finally, the local community is like a *democracy* insofar as its leadership, once conferred by the consent of the governed, is exercised through regular (constitutional) channels. The basis of leadership is support of the group's charism in the Church. Family, brotherhood, and democracy are viable only in proportion to the degree of interpersonal communication and transparency so prized by St. Francis. It is interesting to recall in the context of the last two paragraphs on the common life and the local community an anecdote in the life of St. Francis. In 1209 St. Francis was about to take his small band, under the patronage of Cardinal John Colonna, to see Pope Innocent III. They elected Bernard of Quintavalle, not St. Francis, to lead them. In their democratic family they recognized the superior skills of this knowledgeable brother—whence flowed his obvious leadership in a venture to achieve the next step in validating their charism, that is, hierarchical approval. Thus Bernard played Aaron to the Moses of St. Francis.

Family, brotherhood (or sisterhood), and democracy—these are some dimensions of Franciscan community life. But how are these dimensions retained in a practical way? There is no single formula, of course, but in every social group some criteria need to be maintained to reinforce the common life as far as it is applicable to individual situations. To reduce common life to a mere mental attitude is farcical; without concrete acts as the sign of this attitude, common life begins to fail.

Christ sent his Apostles forth "two by two"—but from some base of operations, to which they returned to make their reports to him. Similarly, St. Francis sent his brothers forth from the friary "like pilgrims and strangers in the world" (*First Rule*, Chapter Six), to work with their hands, to seek alms, to preach with simple exhortation. The friary was a springboard into secular society; to the friary they returned for rest and spiritual refreshment. Their state was obviously fluid, but the thrust of their lives was to hurry back to their communities. It is this allegiance that is the final support of home life, fraternity, and democracy. Those who are without such allegiance are using the friary or convent for a hotel.

It is not that a totally simultaneous life is the important thing, nor should one wish to be immersed into a super-sized community. Number, of course, is related to compatibility of the members and the apostolates of the community. If we trust the Vatican II documents (*Decree on the Ministry and Life of Priests*), then the Eucharistic celebration is the source and root of community life for every Christian group. The point here is to be realistic without, on the other hand, totally canceling the common prayer life. One meal a day toward evening, shared in relaxation with our co-religious and cronies, is the social reinforcement of what occurs at Mass. A typical day should include these three elements to some minimal degree: the Eucharist, a common meal, and spontaneous recreation.

Obviously there are even long periods when individual members are off on business or holiday; this fact does not preclude the common life. But the frame of reference of our activities is the ideal community into which we draw the less outgoing members and give evidence of transparency to them ourselves. No community survives unless the members are accessible to each other's needs and actually communicate, not just pretend. Without some common "exercises" there is simply no possibility for encounter with the group as a group— it would be like belonging to a union and never attending meetings, socials, or voting.

A religious community exists for the Church's mission, but it also presents itself to the world in a way that benefits the members. One practical spiritual application in St. Francis' mind is that the first apostolate of the community is to itself. Members sanctify one another by their helpfulness. Christ's primary activity in his public life was to sanctify and form his Apostles into a believing and worshiping community by example and correction. St. Francis remarked (*First Rule*, Chapter Five) that if a brother lives according to the flesh rather than the spirit, his confreres should humbly, but diligently warn, instruct, and correct the erring brother. In Chapter Seven he goes on to tell his followers to respect and honor each other for a spiritual reason and not to murmur against a confrere.

Let us make a brief application of the statements of the present chapter to a community of eight Franciscan sisters teaching in a parish school. The large and expensive parish convent would be unnecessary. A modest wage—probably much less than that paid to lay teachers—would support the sisters' renting of two apartments in the locale of their teaching. St. Francis' dislike of owning property and living pretentiously or apart from people would thus be adequately expressed. Despite the raise in salary, the parish would gain by not having to buy land, build and maintain a convent. Religious would learn the value of money and the need to live like their neighbors. If Franciscan sisters (one cannot speak for the charism of others) were to gravitate to the parishes with higher standards and salaries, the whole believing community would recognize (and rightly scoff at) their low-grade charism. The sisters would worship before and after school in the parish church—no insignificant witness in itself. This brand of common life and mobile structure applies as readily to nursing and social-service sisters. Meanwhile the major superior would visit the sisters often to support their ventures and see to their needs. (Houses of formation are considered separately below.)

The result of the free-wheeling behavior of St. Francis is that our Order fosters a spirit of greater spontaneity than many other institutes, but this fact is not always apparent in Franciscan history. Nevertheless, the complexities of ancient restrictions never quite destroyed the idea that "Franciscan" suggests informality, hospitality, good cheer, and the family spirit. The absence of regimentation and, ideally, the accessibility of superiors should permit the individuality of a Franciscan to increase. The hallmark of the Franciscan is to be a *bon vivant* in the religious sense and within the framework of the vows, without becoming an "oddball."

As St. Paul described it, we ought to have the "glorious freedom of the children of God" (Romans 8:21). This excludes the notion of living under a tyrant. It bespeaks a sense of filiation and family spirit with God, not with human beings alone. But freedom by itself has a negative description; it is the "absence of some restriction." St. Paul's idea is positive; law is *internalized and self-imposed*. No religious is ever free to be the unique individual God calls him to become, until he no longer *needs* prohibitions laid upon him. The paradox of Christianity is that only the unfree person needs the burden of law. Hence the writer of the Epistle says that those who had lived under the law of Moses had a heavy burden, but by their adoption into God's family as Christians they become free by reason of the love-relationship, which is the primary "command" of the New Testament.

The internalization of law is never likely to occur if it does not happen in the houses of formation. There is seldom much similarity between them and "real-life" houses, however. Houses of formation should be small enough to prevent any candidate's submersion in numbers. They are no place to send senior members who are disturbed by and critical of the apparently erratic behavior of the young. They should not be made a refuge for derelicts, penitents, the mentally ill, and those incapable of living peacefully anywhere else. How can an authentic community be built up? Houses of formation do need older members, but with great flexibility and charity to provide the important example of joyful maturity. In the dreadful and un-Franciscan super-communities of some sisters—consisting of aspirants, postulants, novices, scholastics, senior sisters, and what-not—the only way to reconcile the situation is to give each group a sense of identity through the appointment of separate superiors, independence of action, and liturgies to suit the participants—under separate chaplains, if possible. This ideal is often impractical as houses of formation are presently set up, but they should be planned for the future. Most Franciscans will not live in huge houses after formation; hence their training is unrealistic if the Constitutions and lectures present one standard and the apostolate another. How much worse it is when houses of formation are elaborate and cater to the young when the professed live in comparative squalor.

The novitiate is a period of self-analysis and some sequestration, but it cannot be totally unrelated to the apostolate and separate from the other houses of the province. Novices should travel to other houses which are near enough and even remain there a day or two to observe. This does not violate the integrity of a canonical year if it does not exceed three months. (*Instruction on the Renewal of Religious Formation* (United States Catholic Conference, 1969), pp. 14f.) They should see the alcoholics, the sick, and the "oddballs"— whether they are priests or brothers or sisters. The local religious could explain their ministry and answer the frank questions of the young. Thus the principles enunciated in training could be given a more realistic setting.

The last paragraph refers, of course, to a novitiate year which comes prior to wearing the habit and taking first vows. In the institutes which now place the novitiate at the end of the total formation program—for the priest, before he has received major orders; for the sister, after she has been on mission in a few other houses of the province. Probably the most desirable time for a person to enter the novitiate is at the point where, after adequate counseling, he or she feels the need to prepare for the total commitment of final vows, whenever that might occur during formation. To avoid caprice and disruption of an apostolate, the candidate could give a year's notice, at which time, however, the major superior might request some compromise for the good of the province.

In Franciscan history it often seemed that the formation process was successful if the individual had reached a total conformity with traditional behavior patterns, particularly those of thought. Now we realize that formation is successful only when the *individual* emerges enough to support the community charism with his or her special talents. St. Paul taught us that *every* Christian has a particular gift to offer the community. Celano puts these words into the mouth of St. Francis: "God does not cater to special individuals. The minister general of the Order, who is the Holy Spirit, settles upon a poor and simple person as easily as upon another" (Celano, *Second Life*). Counterfeit "gifts" of the Spirit are generally obvious. When one brother was applauded for not breaking silence by even going to confession, St. Francis called it rather a gift of the devil. And when a young brother groaned during his sleep because of hunger pains after excessive fasting, St. Francis wakened him to have a full meal and an object lesson.

The satisfaction of a Franciscan in his ministerial role should not be founded on his environment. Once granted the freedom to do his work reasonably well, the strong religious should *ideally* transcend the onus of the common life, such as irritating personalities, a suspicious superior, minimal living standards, and a lack of time for reflection and relaxation. *Realistically* one's total environment is a conditioner of his role satisfaction. In a house of formation, however, one's self-concept flows almost totally from intra-community factors: recognition by authority, acceptance to the next level of training, emergence of the individual through attempts at self-expression in a non-threatening environment, the perception of growth through learning, and so forth. Because of the only limited apostolate possible to trainees, the "feedback" that is supportive of one's own worth and relevance is derived almost completely from the common life. For this last reason above all, in a house of formation *individuation occurs by means of the common life.*

The training process must allow, even encourage, the deviations from itself that bring about the very goals for which the process exists. Although maximum use of personal talents is desirable, nevertheless, insofar as charism must be guided by authority for the good of the whole group, this is not always possible in any life, not only religious life. The excruciating frustration of one's *activities* does not necessarily cause the frustration of one's *inner growth*, both psychologically and spiritually. Nevertheless, those persons consistently incapable of such frustration should not remain in religious life. Nor should those remain who are unfit for the joyful burden of obedience—for grudging obedience is a caricature of religious life. If superiors, on the other hand, habitually "test" subjects or prefer the letter of the law to its spirit during the period of formation, the process of individuation is retarded, possibly even stopped, because the candidate develops a whole set psychologically crippling responses in order to survive in religious life.

Loyalty to the institute does not necessarily mean conformity. To love the Order one should be willing to risk everything, including personal disgrace or crucifixion, to improve it. Religious, insofar as they represent an officially sanctioned modality of the Gospel life, should be freed to become what nature and grace have indicated. Education and formation should be flexible enough to give the young religious the conviction that he is trusted and is mature enough to develop within the greater context of the Franciscan charism. Candidates generally enter religious life with a docile spirit; they are eager to serve God and man through the institute. They trust the insights of older religious until they "learn" that conformity, mindless obedience, and exterior religiosity seem to be rewarded in their organization. Individuality is called "singularity." Friendship is suspect. Originality is reckoned as divisive. Meanwhile Franciscan optimism and romanticism and freedom of emotional expression are left to the biographies of St. Francis and sermons to the laity.

Age and experience deserve respect, not for their own sake, but because they presume maturity and wisdom apart from the tally of years. The Spirit, however, does not confine itself to age brackets. It speaks to everyone who is willing to listen. An institute or province divided into factions by *aggiornamento* is wasting its time on dialogue and self-study and updating. If the segregation of minds is that complete, with nobody in the middle, the love-relationship which is the pulse of the community is already defunct. If anything destroys individuation, it is having the viewpoint of the stronger imposed on the weaker, regardless of who may finally be proved correct by history.

The customs taught to young religious should not be imposed, but proposed as the typical behavior of seasoned religious. But if there is a double standard, and the older sisters, brothers, and priests do not live by the so-called customs and ascetical practices, they were surely unreal in the first place. The style of life of young religious should grow out of observing older religious. Otherwise it would seem that the final results in the conduct of older persons do not justify the training "process" and the multiplicity of regulations.

The individuation of a Franciscan is never complete when he lives a merely useful life. This could be only good citizenship and great humanitarianism. He must have loving sonship and the continuing contact of prayer to live a full life. One does not need a long life to have a full life. To have lived a full life is to have lived long enough. In order to become a fully actualized person with his potentials brought to the surface, one needs the liberating action of personhood and prayer. Personhood is not a static summation of qualities or achievements. Personhood is a dynamic state, characterized by the capacity for *change* (the sign of growth) and *self-expression* (the sign of uniqueness).

St. Francis was such a total person. Therefore, he gave himself to others, expended physical effort to live the apostolic life, even at the cost of his own health, as we recall from his increasing blindness and stomach disease. He communicated his intellectual and emotional life by passionately proposing his innovations and idealism to the scrutiny of the Church and the world. He shared his spiritual life by giving us his prayers, confessing his weaknesses, and bringing us to his awareness of the human Christ. The ability to expose oneself is a sign of maturity, for it subjects the ego to the risk of rejection by others, which often happened to Francis. The strong supernatural faith of St. Francis reinforced his naturally strong ego in the presentation of his charism to other men and women.

Another way of asserting this statement is that we are always trying to crash the gates of paradise and return to the womb in which we were corporately formed. Genesis describes paradise as a place of orderliness, harmony with nature, no distortion of truth, correct relationships, abundance of food, ease of learning, and work as a joy to the heart. A careful reading of the creation story certifies all these elements. Every man longs for that paradise from which he is an exile. In the Jungian sense of *archetype*, paradise looks back and beckons us forward. It is both the point of origin and place of return; where we started and wither we end. Note that we (at least First World nations) are achieving some of these goals during the close of the 20th century: abundance of food, ease of learning through computer networking, work as a joy through automation, technology as mastery over nature, and so forth.

As soon as there were enough individuals to constitute common life, the process of individuation asserted its negative valence within the equation; our relationships with God and each other unbalanced the common life. Sin entered the story, and individuals began to accuse one another. "The woman you gave me made me do it," said Adam. "That snake in the tree seduced me," retorted Eve, at first the mother of the living and now the mother of all who would die. So the angel with the flaming sword stands at the gate and forbids us entry until our relationships are corrected—at the end of time. In fact, we shall discover that the angel has disappeared, because paradise will have extended its perimeter to the ter-

minus of the world itself. Then the process of individuation
will serve the commonality, not divide it, as commonly occurs. Meanwhile we are a people wandering on exodus, on
pilgrimage, homeless, called to a new covenant like Abraham,
whereby we leave the familiar, own opinions and desires, accept new ideas, new life styles, new assignments and bailiwicks. Like the onions and leeks of Egypt, sometimes the
very recollection of our successes, friendships, even the past
glories of the Order imprison us in the past.

In the embolism of the Mass we pray, "we wait in joyful
hope" (not looking back to some elusive Eden, not sighing
with nostalgia for the "good old days"). Remember the days
of scholasticism and medieval universalism in the Church; we
were told that the thirteenth was the greatest of centuries, as
if human history moved backwards since then, and God was
helpless to advance it. The eminent French writer is quoted
as saying, "The Middle Ages were an immense Church such
as will not be seen again until God returns to earth, a place of
prayer as vast as the entire West, and built on ten centuries of
ecstasy which recall the Ten Commandments of Sabaoth."
Bloy completely overlooked the barbarians, the superstitious,
the heavy-handed sanctions of the Church, feudal slavery, and
the outside plumbing.

Individuation could not occur when the individuals were
encapsulated in "Sunday ideas," as I recall Bertrand Russell
used to call them. These are the pious, comfortable thoughts
you are likely to hear from the pulpit about the wickedness of
our time—which are not realistic, practical, or theological
when you test them out on weekdays. Nevertheless I confess
to occasional secret triumphalism that glances backward to
when the catechisms were uniform, patriotism was sure, and
theological opinion was univocal—and safely in Latin. I sigh
over Gothic carvings stored in Church basements. Once we
called it "bragging," now it's "giving witness." Formerly it
was "shooting off your mouth," now we call it "transpar-

ency." Before we rationalized idiosyncrasies; now the idiosyncrasies have become charisms. These are "Sunday ideas."

If individuation will continue to succeed, then the "Sunday ideas" about the danger of change and experiment must
be laid aside. Experiment is supposed to be perilous and shake
us free from the comfortable and predictable and familiar.
Remember how the pope and his curia felt about St. Francis'
wanting to live the Gospel as Jesus did! "Does that mean
Jesus gave us an impossible command to fulfill an unrealistic
ideal?" the Founder queried them. The Spirit blew where it
chose, and the curia capitulated. (It must have been in between Sundays!)

Perhaps we are yet in the early stages of Christianity
and of the Franciscan Order. Theologians tell us the Church
was born out of the side of Christ on Calvary and reached
maturity on Pentecost. I am sure that all the facilities and
capacities and charisms were present, but not the Church's
corporate emotional security. My personal fantasy is that
during those risky days of *infancy* the Church depended utterly on God the Spirit, not reflecting too intensively on the
contents of faith, and expecting the imminent return of Jesus,
the *parousia*, so they lived with a sense of catastrophe that
often invade children's lives, as the age of infancy.

As the official religion of the Empire, the orthodox bishops rightly warred without compromise with its *sibling ri-
vals*, the various heresies. The Church's medieval, simplistic
pre-adolescence, was narrow and confined to European feudal thought patterns; inflexible, with everything clearly black
or white, delighting in mechanical formulas that sounded
unshakeable. The *early adolescent* Renaissance, conscious of
its budding physical and mental powers, felt strictured by the
previous generation, so looked to fulfillment and values of
the world. The full-blown *adolescent rebellion of Protestant-
ism* against the parent church reached extremes of violence so
that many good forms of religious expression were also aban-

doned as well, and the Church hardened its heart against its wayward children.

The religious history of this metaphor during the past four centuries is ever more complex, but perhaps we are reaching some compromise (not doctrinally) and maturity in our pluralistic society. Instead of a standoff, as in an inconclusive battle, perhaps we can learn to be like the householder of the faith, who brings out of his storehouse old things and new, and seek out paradise again, both backwards and forwards. At least we can take a lesson from Lucifer and his angels: by arguing over paradise they lost it. Feelings and bias were never reasoned into an individual, therefore they cannot be reasoned out of a person either!

There are many "Sunday ideas" that do *not* prove out during the week and we ought not let them inhibit our process of individuation within the common life....

1. The feeling of older religious that their past efforts were foolish or useless, in vain without religious value, their prayers, adorations, fasts, being home by six or eight or ten o'clock, strictly timed meditations, customs of the Order observed by 20 or more years was an empty ritual that never pleased God.

2. The "Sunday" pious feeling that our Order is growing weaker spiritually—fewer prayers means a lesser bargaining power with God, so to speak.

3. Religious are losing the protection to virtue offered by the habit, going about two by two, etc. This has become a non-issue for many communities, but those who keep these practices are often made to feel like quaint antiques in the attic of the Church.

4. A feeling of being hurt when older members see how the younger appear to be catered to. They don't have to get their degrees the hard way (after school and on Saturdays) and struggle to pay off community mortgages on motherhouses, convalescent homes, colleges, and so forth.

Superiors will do practically anything to procure and keep vocations, who now want to sell the buildings anyway!

5. As a whole there is a loss of tradition, history, being rooted in the past. From this arises the fear of being abandoned in one's old age. Young and old see little security in their future if everyone is doing his/her own thing.

6. In the past the responsibility for progress and change was in the hands of the few who were elected and "freed" to act mostly through their councils. Now the highest superior is easily approached with innovations, suggestions, challenges and questions. Information was sparingly shared from top to bottom that now is more widely disseminated.

7. Formal and ritualistic patterns of behavior were based on titles and functions and now have ceded to persons rather than process.

8. Age and length of service should be rewarded, but competence is even more significant. In the end, it seemed that docility and conformity were the bases of promotion and approval. Many religious' most "Sunday idea" is to have the Church and Order to be as narrow as their own restricted vision of it. Whereas superiors have the grace of office (a favorite "Sunday" cliche), having a grace and using it are quite different.

9. Always crossing nature is good for the soul. But during the week we see the value of a birthday cake and a swim in the sun. In fact, the "best" way to cross nature is to endure the unexpected phone call, parent, student, or pastor.

10. Formerly if we had permission it was thought we were practicing poverty and obedience. Now we are told to ask Jesus first without trying to manipulate the superior into agreeing with us.

God and the Church do not need our survival; both antedate us and need our prophetism. We are not religious for just our own salvation. No one is "lost" or "saved" alone.

We are *ecclesial* persons. It was easier to live in a two-story universe that didn't overlap too much. The earth belonged to the devil, the "prince of this world," and we were better out of it as soon as possible; meanwhile it was best to ignore earth as long as we were condemned to stay here. The Church was the travel agency between the two stories. As we look back on the process of individuation in the common life, we do well to wonder at the freedom St. Francis bequeathed to us to pursue our individuation. As wonderful as our activities have been, it is the charity, spirit, and other worldliness that we bring to our ministries which give them meaning. Most of all, I think our "work" must bespeak a relationship with God. Now, however, we take the "magic" out of religion, and we are less apt to try to manipulate God to accomplish our goals and win our victories. In a world of skyscrapers, moonwalks, and deep freezes it seems we need the providence of God less and less, but more and more of his friendship and guidance.

As God moves human history to its close, he uses "secular" programs to perfect the City of Man, social programs, civil rights, anti-poverty. Because many of the services that religious provide (as education, counseling, and health care) can be provided equally well by laity, religious Orders have no purpose in the world, unless we give witness that our prayer is profound, our convictions are uncompromising, our heroism absolute, our faith boundless, our hope unshaken. You may never be certain of your meaning and of the point of your vocation in this life. Maybe you are simply meant to be the carrier of hopes to the following generation. And that will be more than enough!

CHAPTER VIII

Secular Franciscans

We have called the Franciscan charism a demonstration that the gospel life can be successfully lived in any condition, places or time of life. It is a call given to men and women, married and celibate, priests and laymen to return to the Apostolic Age of the Church. If this be accurate, it follows that all ranks of mankind should be able to see their particular status in life being fulfilled by Franciscans somewhere and their special problems interpreted for them through the evangelical life. For this reason Franciscans do not claim to *do* something special in the Church, but try to *mean* something special. Teachers, office workers, scientists, parish priests, clowns, cloistered women, mothers, and ditch-diggers should be able to look to Franciscans for a model of the Christ-life within the present moment. To fulfill their charism, Franciscans must penetrate all of society. Historically, the three Orders have attempted this; they remain the largest group in the Church oriented to a single charism. Their degree of success in restoring the creative age of the apostles is subject to debate, of course.

In the *Second Rule*, Chapter Six, the Founder tells his brothers to be "as pilgrims and strangers in this world, serving the Lord in poverty and humility." This does not sound like world-shaking involvement. But one cannot quote a man outside the context of his actions. (We remember that Christ told us to turn our back on father and mother—cf. Luke 14:26). St. Francis' movement was "secular" in contrast to the existing religious life. He did not permit his brothers to live an eremitical life. For those who needed periodic sequestration he provided the *retiro*, with a special rule of life, requiring at least four brothers for this community of silence and prayer. Thus he did not believe that the solitary life was for his followers. In the Chapter at Assisi in 1269, St. Bonaventure decreed that hermits were not to make profession in the Order. As a matter of fact, the original twelve followers of St. Francis came from many walks of life—lawyer, priest, businessman, soldier, peasant. Having known the world, they were better adapted to transform it.

The profane world can become the sacred world, if men make it so. We see this reflected in the poem of St. Francis, *The Canticle of Brother Sun*, in which he calls the world of nature and even Sister Death to praise the Lord God. Similarly a painter, architect, or plumber who is faithful to the truth within him serves the God of truth in the best religious sense; the "maker" is aware of his limitations, respects the materials in his hand, and completes the work of creation by improving the human milieu. In a word, I do not think the Franciscan charism can be defined and clarified without reference to "secularity." The Founder was accustomed to say the Order was a gift for the salvation of the world. As a *movement* its witness and work exceeds the individual ministries of priests and brothers, nuns and sisters.

Before St. Francis secularity was the less-than-best way to serve God, although there were religious and priests who did live among men. They did not work alongside them, however, as did the original followers of St. Francis and the tertiaries after them. Typically, the religious person found God in a cloister; those who gave witness to the dignity of labor wore a Benedictine habit. St. Anselm of Canterbury, the primary medieval spiritual master before St. Francis, kept urging young men to retreat to the monasteries for salvation. Anything else was both folly and useless. Particularly before the great number of priests joined him, St. Francis considered his movement—what was to become the First Order—a layman's recall to the Gospel life. Thus, in the *First Rule*, before he developed his own charism completely, he wrote, "The brothers should occupy themselves in the arts they understand....Each should remain in the skill or craft from which he was called to religious life....And they may keep the tools and instruments necessary for their work" (*First Rule*, Chapter Seven). We remember that, although Christ called a publican and fishermen to leave their occupations, the soldiers and farmers and rich merchants and other laypersons were simply commanded to live justly and in love by St. John the Baptist. St. Francis saw his brothers as the leaven in the lump of dough, mingling with the common folk in their homes and fields and shops. Later, the First Order became specifically apostolic, primarily because the priests, whose "natural" work was preaching, were also to remain in the "craft" from which they had entered the Order. One is inclined to think that the Founder prescribed in the *Second Rule* that the unlearned brother should not be anxious to acquire learning, in order to retard the clericalization of his Order. In any case, it was the Third Order which finally became the lay Franciscan movement and what Francis most desired.

Cloistered Franciscans, such as the Poor Clares, seem to be an enigma with respect to the charism of our Order. In what sense does their community life demonstrate that the evangelical life proposed by Christ in the first century can be successfully lived in any century?

First of all, the cloistered cannot be ignorant of the world's needs—political, social, moral. Their "secularity" or involvement presents a risk to their way of life, but all acts of faith are a risk. The Franciscan cannot be realistically insulated against the world. It may be the charism of a Carmelite nun to sequester herself (she alone can be sure) but not a Franciscan. Involvement means that the Poor Clare monastery should be set in the midst of a city where, like a Christian community of prayer set upon a mountain, everyone, especially the spiritually indigent, can see the life of voluntary poverty, the sharing with the deprived what is given to the convent as alms, and a joyful accessibility for those who come to the parlor.

The disadvantaged, the emotionally disturbed, the despairing should be able to seek out the Clares and also hear a "simple exhortation," receive spiritual comfort, and join in uplifting prayer. The day is here when some Clares should be educated in counseling techniques to aid the poor of Christ. That this has not happened in the past is no reason that it cannot happen in the future, especially women, battered wives, "fallen" women, confused teenaged girls. What a gift to the third millennium of Christianity. So St. John the Baptist counseled those who gathered at the Jordan River for the baptism of repentance. This need not make the monastery a clinic, but a refuge for the theologically and emotionally guilty—a place where no barriers of an appointment, a secretary, questionnaires, and testing programs separate a client from a human encounter in the moment of need. Where are the abbesses who are bold to attempt this ministry?

Hopefully, the inhuman custom of the grille will cease in order to permit authentic face-to-face charity. Thus, although the Clares cannot go among the laity, they can live alongside them. They must learn to be secure in the dysfunctionality of their roles in our age, which measures a person's worth by the tangible results of his activity and his ability to compete for the attention of the world. They proclaim the hope of resurrection better by intimacy with God than by any social hyperactivity. Our Clares make the silent, prayerful, and poor Christ present to the Church and to the world. They, too, are women of joy, optimism, free expression, and romantic idealism. When this is not verified in a convent, it is because the leaders do not trust this spontaneity and this openness to the neighborhood of the monastery. Thus the life of the Poor Clare is an adaptation of the Franciscan charism, in which accessibility is still a dimension of the Gospel, and even secularity is an option.

The non-cloistered, active Franciscan sisters of the various Third Order groups have already been considered in the chapter on community life, particularly with respect to their experimentation and mobility. Just as the Poor Clares were urged to be more accessible to the needy—as, for example, in counseling—tertiary religious ought to seek out the disadvantaged in areas of life where the Gospel has not been adequately demonstrated as the source of religious activity—dope-addiction, suicide-prevention school work, mental retardation, pastoral assistance, senescence. Such groups need a nucleus of religious around which to form a "total-life" Christian community, wherein the hope of resurrection assuages human grief. The religious tertiary is given to the world not just to live a parallel life with the needy nor to enter their lives sporadically. She is not bound to the cloister like the Clare, nor to the altar like a priest, nor to a family like most secular tertiaries. She can, therefore, with her co-religious be the magnet to which the needy gravitate for an experience of total Christian life in new institutional forms. These religious should be "secular" enough to prepare professionally and to use government aid to bring dedication to fields where there exists a danger that persons become only "case histories." Of course, they must beware of seeking glamorous and dramatic apostolates for other than spiritual reasons, and they must give reasonable protection to their cloister and privacy, for the convent is their home.

The final comments on Franciscan secularity are reserved for the group to which they are eminently applicable, the Third Order Secular, the "lay persons" in their home. These men and women are the parade example of Gospel secularity. St. Francis tried not so much to "bring" God to the world as to show that he was already there. In the words of St. Bonaventure, the universe bears the *vestigia*, the "footprints," of God; we must track him down among us, especially in each other. St. Francis neither surrenders to the Secular City nor destroys it; he makes in his Third Order a single habitation for God and man. By improving the world and continuing the work of creation, man sanctifies the universe as his worship of God. But the man who attempts this must first himself be holy and practicing the evangelical counsels. No one can know the Word of God, by whom all things were made and without whom nothing was made, unless the heavenly Father reveals him.

In a sense, the Third Order Secular has represented for seven hundred years a "glorification" of the common man; for he, too, shares in a religious charism and in the religious state. The title of "minors" identifies the First Order members as nonentities in the medieval world; St. Francis even asked Hugolino, the Cardinal Protector, to bring the friars who were seeking preferments and prelacies down to earth (Celano, *Second Life*). The title of "Poor Ladies of St. Damian" originally identified the Second Order as unendowed women living by alms. The Third Order Secular can add to unglamorous and otherwise pedestrian lives the extra spiritual factor of living in obedience to canonical superiors, without property as a status symbol, and in the chastity of married or single life.

Tertiaries are particularly courteous and cheerful, lest there be some "credibility gap" between their profession and life style. They are devoted to the humanity of God's Son.

Their modesty or "continency" in living, homes, clothes, cars, and so forth attests to their following of the poor Christ. They share themselves and their resources (financial, psychological, and spiritual) with others in the fraternity in idealized community life. Optimistically they believe and expect and cause others to rise to a higher level of aspiration. Above all, they have that sense of freedom and transparency of self-expression and joy of life, even in suffering, that is the hallmark of the Franciscan charism. St. Francis' creative approach to religious life permeates their lives as well, so the tertiaries also share in the mandate to return to the Apostolic Age of the Church.

Thus canonized tertiaries have come from all social categories and careers—royalty and peasants, martyrs and penitents, lawyers and businessmen, physicians and blacksmiths. Several founders and foundresses of other institutes began as tertiaries and crystallized their movement into a religious congregation. The Cure' of Ars considered the Third Order the means God intended to elevate parishes morally, and he himself was a tertiary and the only canonized parish priest! King St. Louis of France and Queen St. Elizabeth of Hungary were chosen the chief tertiary patrons, not because of their rank but precisely because, in spite of their rank, they did not idle their lives away uselessly. St. Joan of Arc, a tertiary called by Mark Twain the "genius of disinterested patriotism," became a saint by responding to her inner voices. She was not a martyr to the faith—she was battling another Catholic nation and was condemned by a Church tribunal (or a travesty of one). But she was a "martyr" in the sense of being a "witness"—in her response to the inspiration to unite her nation, which we may call her personal charism. Her austere clothes, hair style, and lack of feminine adornment reflected the Third Order regulations of her century. St. Joan's utterly spiritual and completely secular life became a single involvement with God and man that should typify tertiary life in the world.

Someone has said that God writes straight with crooked

lines. Perhaps it was partly a matter of political expediency that brought the Third Order into eminence very quickly. Cardinal Hugolino, later Gregory IX, wished the tertiaries to take vows in order that they might be exempt from military service, which the medieval serf owed to his lord. Thus the anti-papal Ghibellines would lose an important source of military personnel. Naturally, then, the Third Order was not popular with feudal masters, but its cause was espoused by popes and bishops. The situation of the members was akin to that of the conscientious objectors of subsequent centuries who protested wars they deemed unjustified.

The Third Order is not, therefore, to be just another parish or inter-parish society. It does not merely touch one part of a Catholic's life nor simply add an extra chore; it is a new way of life. But evidence of the *public profession* of the Gospel must be restored to tertiaries. They have their habit, but it is not visible in modern life. They have a fraternal community, but its apostolate is not very often the compelling example of the Christ-life that it ought to be. A Rule, Constitutions, novitiate, profession, and visitation give them a canonical structure. Their office and spiritual conferences give them a liturgical community. Yet their charism as a group is not always evident to the Church and to the world. It is easy enough to say that the testimony of a good life is enough identification. But insofar as Franciscans are given by God for the salvation of the world, tertiaries must demonstrate the Gospel in lay life more visibly and not just as an appendage or mere lay affiliate of the First Order. This latter viewpoint is reinforced in the minds of Franciscan priests by the very brevity of the "course" in Third Order direction given them, like an afterthought in their seminary days.

The Third Order laypersons, who once pronounced religious vows, are an important, even an essential part of the total Franciscan charism, since the Apostolic Age obviously consisted more of lay persons than of priests and of consecrated women. First Order priests are chaplains and creators

of liturgical community, but members of the fraternity themselves should propose, decide, and lead the group according
to their inspirations. The chaplain (who can be a diocesan
priest) is the liaison with the hierarchy, which preserves the
orthodoxy and mission of the Church. He is the spiritual
adviser of *collegia poenitentium*, or "gatherings of penitents,"
as tertiaries were sometimes called. Besides presiding over
the liturgical community, which is the source and root of the
social-action community (*Decree on the Ministry and Life of
Priests*), the chaplain counsels the individuals to the measure
of their existing potential to apply the Gospel to their careers,
family lives, budgets, and apostolate. He visits the homes of
the ailing members and those who live too far away to attend
the meetings. He avoids overwhelming them with his personality and directives that the members are too paralyzed to act
out their own insights. He gives them the attitude of
continentium, another word used by St. Francis. It can be
translated "abstainers," "self-disciplined," or "those who
withhold themselves" from the world while not rejecting the
world. Because of the lack of priests and sisters to form and
spiritually direct tertiaries, the process of "regionalization" is
expected to aid the growth of the Third Order Secular Franciscans. "Regionalization" means smaller fraternities are
grouped into geographically-based units to use personnel more
wisely and not duplicate educational and spiritual programs
within the groups.

We know precious little about the relationship of the
Founder with the first tertiaries. But we can have ample understanding of how he would have acted toward them. In
fact, Paul Sabatier saw in Francis' *Letter to All the Faithful* a
kind of rule for his spiritual sons and daughters, the "brothers and sisters of penance." Of the nearly 40 manuscripts of
the *letter* coming down from the medieval period none of them
makes explicit to whom the *letter* was addressed. Nevertheless, it really was not meant, as the title bespeaks, for *all* the
faithful, but for those to whom Francis owed some direction

and leadership, "those who are living religiously." The addressees of this letter are somehow called to follow the Master in a special way; "we must observe the precepts and counsels of our Lord Jesus Christ," living according to the Gospel. They were bound together in fraternities under their own superiors, to whom they had promised obedience. So this *Letter to (All) the Faithful* is a necessary prolegomenon in understanding tertiary life and their rule.

It is rather amazing that St. Francis, never a professional theologian, typically brings up deeply theological matters in his "popular" letters. So in this *Letter to (All) the Faithful*, Francis attacks the current heresies, especially Catharism, which considered matter as evil, created by the devil. This implies that the Incarnate Jesus himself could scarcely be good or divine, and that the Eucharist must be unreal! Francis returns to his frequent theme of the necessity of the sacramental priesthood. Other admonitions underscore poverty, and disinterested service to others. These factors show the Franciscan charism at work: service and preaching, plus demonstrating that the Gospel can be radically lived by anyone, anywhere, anytime, the important lesson for Secular Franciscans.

One of the most important "signs" of secularity that Franciscans often lack in our time is *dysfunctionality*, that strange contradiction seldom well understood in an age when productivity, excellence and status seem to be everyone's proper goal. Within the desirable achievement of Franciscan visibility and secularity there always remains the special meaning of being a "sign of contradiction to the world," namely, that we best influence this world's values by opposing them as Christ and Francis did in their centuries. "What we utter is God's wisdom: a mysterious, hidden wisdom" (I Cor. 2:6). "God has revealed this wisdom to us through the Spirit....We speak not in words of human wisdom, but in words taught by the Spirit." The Spirit teaches us to still the strident voices of the world's values and to listen to Jesus.

"Secularity" must remain part of the Franciscan dream, otherwise, we remain a mystery to ourselves, without focus, pattern, or framework. Tertiaries, already familiar with the world about them, know about "fathering," building up a citizenry that defends practical values; about "mothering," nurturing a family that stands together against adversity; and now about "brothering," forming a universal democracy of equals before God in the new secularity.

To father, mother, and brother is the *mission* of secularity (which is kind of the reverse side of the coin of charism). On February 24, 1208 Francis heard the Gospel of Matthew 10 about going on mission. The Gospel he had heard many times he finally listened to. Then he preached his first sermon at San Giorgio (where later he and St. Clare were first buried) on the topic of repentance, because the Kingdom of God was at hand. In recapturing the springtime of the Church and its mission, Francis found twelve apostles and allowed numerous groups of disciples to find him, which were the Secular Franciscans.

They went first to the lost sheep of the House of Israel, Catholics in danger of heresy, as the Albigensians. They announced the reign of God with healing miracles of body and soul. They lived "off the land," simply, with nothing of their own. If people were unwilling to listen, then the tertiaries were to shake the dust from their sandals, because they had not been on "holy land." They were to avoid contention and persecution, but be glad when they suffered harassment, because Jesus suffered first. They were to speak in full daylight and even from the housetops. This was the ideal for the tertiaries, although most members of families were not mobile enough to experience this radical taste of the Gospel.

The first "secular" disciples of the Founder, as in the case of Jesus, were personal friends. We especially recall Jacopa Settesoli, who was widowed at 22 and mother of two sons to be raised. Francis stayed with her in Rome. In the great basilica of Assisi her portrait has often been mistaken for St.

Clare's, but her escutcheon (or "logo") appears around her picture: seven suns or *settesoli*. As he lay dying, Francis asked that she attend him and bring almond paste confections, *marzipan*. Jacopa raised a pet lamb for Francis and apparently provided him with habits. She is buried at the opposite end of the crypt chapel where the Founder himself lies. Although the honor of being the earliest tertiaries generally goes to a husband and wife, Luchesio and Buona Donna, or to another pair, Elzear and Delphine, I believe the first Secular Franciscan was truly Jacopa.

There is evidence that Cardinal Hugolino helped Francis write a tentative Third Order Rule about 1221 for the Lombard Humiliati, who may have been converting from the heresy to orthodox Catholicism. The original document, however, is lost. I think research may one day show that this Rule may share the wording of his *Letter to (All) the Faithful*, written about the same time.

More than moderns might imagine, there was a need to regulate Third Order life. The classless society envisioned by Francis had political overtones. Their oath-taking took them out of the feudal system of military service, even as conscientious objectors. The requirement of wills and testaments, especially for the wealthier members, prevented altercations among heirs. At the same time the popes granted canonical exemptions and immunities to Secular Franciscans. In addition, there was a surprising degree of ostentation and rivalry in the dress, jewelry and personal possessions, particularly in the fifteenth and sixteenth centuries, as evidenced by the sumptuary laws of Tuscany. St. Francis called for simplicity in dress and ornamentation. An English chronicler, Henry Knighton, noted the pride of even the common folk, that one could scarcely distinguish the poor from the rich, the servant from the master, or a priest from other men.

No doubt Francis learned about the vanity of earthly clothing at his merchant father's knee. The wealthy deplored this imitation of their life style by newcomers who seemed to violate God's seeming plan for a "natural" hierarchy. The sumptuary laws described "exact gradations of fabric, color, fur trimming, ornaments, and jewels for every rank and income level. Efforts were also made to regulate how many dishes could be served at meals, what garments and linens could be accumulated for a trousseau, how many minstrels at a wedding party" (K. Tuchman, *A Distant Mirror.*).

Thus the Franciscan secularity must be deduced from Francis' own actions and few written statements, sometimes enjoined by the popes if only to control and spiritually exploit this lay movement. That same year of 1221 during which the above-cited documents appeared, Francis composed his *memoriale propositi,* "outline (or) memorandum of a proposed way of life." Pope Honorius III issued a papal brief to the Bishop of Rimini, to whom he recommended the "penitents" of Faenza. By 1228 the *memoriale* was amended and added to. Because Hugolino, the Cardinal Protector, had a legalistic bent of mind (as appeared in some sections of the *Rule of 1223*), the *memoriale* is modeled on the existing trade unions or guilds. Debts had to be paid and illegally acquired property returned. Lethal weapons were forbidden. They did not make oaths of loyalty to the towns and communes when tertiaries stood for public office, thus obviating the choice between Guelph and Ghibelline partisanship. As in centuries past tertiaries are still expected to contribute to a common fund and attend the funerals of members.

Before his demise in 1881 Karl Marx compared early Christianity with communist values. The first-century Christians awaited the imminent destruction of the world, at least the Empire of Rome. Engels noted that both movements made a millenarian appeal. And in the thirteenth century there was the mystical Joachim of Flora; the Spirituals and Fraticelli were fixed on Francis as Christ returned to earth and the final age of the Holy Spirit.

I consider the following quote the highest tribute paid to St. Francis in the twentieth century. Lenin wrote this in his

Letters on Modern Atheism.   "I made a mistake. Without doubt, an oppressed multitude had to be liberated. But our method only provoked further oppression and atrocious massacres. My living nightmare is to find myself lost in an ocean of red with the blood of innumerable victims. It is too late now to alter the past, but what was needed to save Russia were ten Francis' of Assisi."

If the secularity of Francis had joined the revolution of Lenin (and Engels and Marx), history might have been written differently at the close of the second millennium.

CHAPTER IX

Franciscan Prayer Life

Christ is present whenever two or more are gathered in his name, whether at prayer or in other godly actions, including eating, studying, recreation. But he is pre-eminently present in the commemorative sacrifice and meal. All forms of common prayer should bear a close relationship to this eminent presence of Christ in the Eucharist. Actually one should not make a radical cleavage between "official" and "non-official," because God's family is in action in either case. Liturgy has a broad meaning; its first translation is "the public business," or "the community in action." The praise of God and thanksgiving thus remain the first order of business, in which the presence of Christ can have several dimensions.

Because the presence of Christ is more obvious and effective in the liturgy, the *praying community* initiates the spiritual bond between persons. It gives energy and formulation to the Christian *social community*, which is the face-to-face group of household, parish, or friary with which one has stable contact. Out of it evolves the *serving community*. Concisely stated, after their encounter with God at worship, wherein the members gratefully consecrate the bread and wine, they turn to each other and to the world, wherein they gratefully consecrate man's secular activities. "Gratitude" is one translation of *Eucharistia*. They remember that it was at the Last Supper that Jesus remarked, "I am in your midst as the one who serves you" (Luke 22:27), and that he washed his apostles' feet.

He prays well during the liturgy who shares in the *action* of the congregation. This is the "horizontal" approach to God, of which we hear so much. The worshipers enter the procession, sing, rise, and respond. They reflect upon and try to share in the sentiments being proclaimed in the rite. But this is generally non-emotional; hence it leaves some worshipers unsatisfied, accustomed as they may be to more affectivity in prayers. Nevertheless, even though these liturgical actions are official and do not rise spontaneously from the worshiper's emotional investment, one supposes that they demonstrate and provide for joy, love, enthusiasm, gratitude, sorrow, filial fear. The silences during the liturgy give some opportunity for communing with God informally and for deeper emotional involvement. This is the "vertical" prayer, made individually to God, which is the norm of private prayer and reflection away from the group. Vertical prayer has a stronger emotional tone, because one discusses with God such matters as career, family, the future, personal sinfulness, specific anxieties.

We remember that St. Francis called himself a "poor little worm" in one of the prayers attributed to him. Although this phrase very nearly echoes David's (Psalm 22, verse 7), describing the sufferings of the virtuous man and also prophesying the role of the Messiah, in itself such a passage is inadequate as a phrase in common prayer, because the partici-

pants cannot be sincere without some feeling of self-deprecia-
tion at a given moment. Each worshiper must accurately discern, in private communion with God, what best expresses
his passing need. This distinction seems essential in drawing
up the ceremonials and books of prayers for a religious institute. Otherwise the merely personal and transitory prayers
of religious founders are thrust upon generations of followers. Incidentally, with respect to "poor little worm," as a
continuing self-concept, it would be suspect in any prayer.

All prayer should be geared to action or change, whether
in the individual's behavior or in the community's service. This
is analogous in the personal life of any religious with his vow
of celibate chastity. The person is freed to love God without
distraction—but that is insufficient. The celibate, man or
woman, is wedded to the Church just as Christ is wedded to
the Church. The virgin can love all the individuals of the community equally and intensively in his or her love of God. The
daily renewal of this particular vow is a prayer that leads to
social action.

Contemporary liturgical reformers remind us to make
all forms of prayer, especially group prayer, conform with the
varying seasonal Eucharistic liturgy—whence the development
of Bible vigils, the administration of sacraments during Mass,
and the paraliturgies, or prayer practices associated with the
liturgy. St. Francis, like most men of faith, accurately saw the
Eucharist as the focus of Catholic life. He revered priests,
including unworthy ones, precisely because they consecrated
and administered the Body of Christ. From his deathbed he
wrote letters to the minister general and to the whole world
about the reverence due to the Blessed Sacrament. He makes
a similar reference in his final Testament. Early in his religious life he chose France as his preaching territory (1217)
because of the respect for the Eucharist there. He frequently
directed his brothers to sweep out and adorn churches as the
true house of God. He was accustomed along the road to
turn toward the nearest tabernacle when he was unable to

reach a church for the time of prayer. At Greccio, the scene of the first Christmas crib, he placed a host on an altar stone that was set in the crib—as a kind of paraliturgy. Similarly, as he lay dying at the Portiuncula, he blessed and broke bread for the brothers who attended him.

The viability of any liturgical community depends on a reasonably small size—perhaps no more than thirty—which generally obtains in religious houses or the Third Order fraternity. Larger communities should break up often into smaller groups based on mutual ties of age, apostolate, and the like. Spontaneous prayer life is more comfortable in such a setting. According to the limits of their apostolates, First Order priests should build up community by concelebration; at least one evening a week should be sacrosanct for concelebration of Mass and the sharing of dinner and recreation. Truthfully, in the early days of the Order, the multiplication of "private" Masses was frowned upon, and even today community may be better expressed by the "conventual" Mass when the group gathers around one celebrant only for Eucharist. Although community spirit is primarily an attitude, it does not long survive without concrete expression. Religious brothers and sisters of our Orders, who do not actively *form* communities of Christians, as do the priests by their ministry, should nevertheless *build up* the community of the apostolate—students, neighbors, the sick, their spiritual clients. (This was emphasized in the chapter on community life. It is reiterated here as a part of Franciscan prayer life.)

Our members should be as free as St. Francis to express themselves in contemporary forms of liturgy—the dialogue homilies, spontaneous prayers, and petitions in the Prayer of the Faithful. In group meditations no one should be forced to contribute; then again, no one ought to be fearful of offering an insight or conviction. In paraliturgies, such as the Chapter of Faults, members can take the occasion to apologize for unkindnesses. To expose one's emotional life is the keenest risk a person can take, for he does not have weapons with which he can defend himself, as in physical or intellectual risks. Perhaps it is better to chance the occasional excesses of some persons rather than stifle self-expression in the cause of the sobriety which may be just this side of indifference. In all these matters of "experiment" and "transparency," a person must be judged in the context of his whole spiritual life insofar as it is apparent—zeal for souls, kindliness to others, theological orthodoxy, faithfulness to the Franciscan charism. If an individual finds little good in existing prayer forms, if he feeds his ego by being *avant-garde*, if he surrounds himself with a "fan club," one has reason also to doubt his genuine transparency.

The prayer life of an institute should express its charism and not be a mere aggregation of the personal whims of past and present superiors. Reducing the number of prayers is not the whole point, either. Ceremonies of investiture, profession, renewal of vows, traditional paraliturgies, and so forth reinforce an Order's self-concept or existential personality. Franciscan prayer life should revolve about the concepts of being "minors," of reliving the Apostolic Age, of the humanity of Christ, of local apostolates, of freedom of self-expression, of optimism about man's perfectibility, of joy in the created world, of poverty, of true secularity, and of serving the disadvantaged. Our three Orders need to develop these concepts even in the Mass by the choice of readings. They should seek permission to substitute such Franciscan elements as a Preface based on the *Canticle of Brother Sun* and a Canon using parts of St. Francis' paraphrase of the Our Father, or the long prayer in Chapter Twenty-three of the *First Rule*. The liturgical greeting could be "The Lord give you peace," which our founder says was directly revealed to him by God. The final benediction might be the blessing of St. Francis to Brother Leo, which is the prayer of the high priest in the Pentateuch (Num. 6:24ff.) already used in the Mass.

It was mentioned earlier in this chapter that sentiment, not sentimentality, is crucial in Franciscan prayer life. Our men have traditionally been popular preachers with a simple, down-to-earth style; thus their ministry has been informed by their prayer life. The best way to be sure of one's hierarchy of values is not by an intellectual process, but by discerning the matters about which one feels strongly. One can apply this norm to prayer also. Whom do you love? What do you fear? Where do you find joy? How is your enthusiasm kindled? What goals give you satisfaction? Which accomplishments have brought you most peace and inner repose? Prayers which never have the support of an emotion (apart from the obvious fact that many persons do not easily verbalize or demonstrate emotions *externally*) may not touch the areas of one's sincere values, but only those which we think we ought to have, because they have been imposed by the Order, by society, or by the exigencies of an apostolate to which we are not fully committed. Secular tertiaries must understand this, too.

Any comments about Franciscan prayer life would be incomplete without mentioning its simplicity. Except for the days of retreat and the novitiate, our prayer life eschews that kind of introspection and self-analysis which bespeak an overemphasis on the ego. We do not classify ourselves in the illuminative way, the seventh interior castle, or the twelfth rung of the ladder. We gravitate to simple ejaculatory prayer and the prayer of quiet gaze or self-disciplined contemplation, for which all forms of prayer are a preparation.

"My mind is so filled with Scriptural passages," St. Francis claimed, "that it has enough for prayer and reflection. I do not need anything beyond what I know about the poor crucified Christ" (Celano, *Second Life*). His Rule prescribed a shorter form of the Divine Office than that used by the monks; unlettered brothers were to recite Our Fathers. Beyond this and the Mass, each brother was left to the inspiration of God. The breviary and Mass provided spiritual reading; meditation needed no prescribed hours. At that time this was true of the monastic Orders as well. In subsequent centuries, when the nature as well as the language of liturgical prayer was slowly forgotten by the majority, priests and lay people multiplied popular devotions in order to feel some contact with God and his saints. How useful and relevant these are to modern Franciscans must be assessed by the individual. Thus the Way of the Cross with formulary prayers might be useful for a group from time to time, but private reflection at the Stations appears to be a better meditation.

One biographer tells of the simplicity of St. Francis' prayer life. He could apparently pass a whole night with the aspiration "My God and my all!" Although Christian prayer life *begins* with immersion in the humanity of Christ as the means of knowing the Father, it does not necessarily end in Christ. The Son sends some rare persons forward for brief encounters with their heavenly Father. They must surrender their anthropomorphisms in order to enter the black emptiness of the indescribable God. At such times the human imagination has no proper object, and the humanity of Christ does not mediate the direct encounter with God. The inner mystery of the Divine Persons touches a person at this point; and it is the Word, rather than the Word-made-flesh, with whom the human person must identify to become a child of the heavenly Father. At such a moment the life of God is not in a man so much as the man is in the life of God. Of course, one must continually return to the Word-made-flesh as the support and center of the spiritual life processes, because mystical moments pass quickly in the workaday world. In our Seraphic Father we see the ultimate of both forms of prayer: the stigmata, from identification with Christ; and the ecstasy of direct, wordless contact with the Father, who cannot be apprehended by any categories of the senses.

The relationship of an Order's prayer life with its charism is somewhat complex, especially after the last quarter-century of growth, change, insight, and post-conciliar statements. (One hopes that all religious institutes pursue this relationship.) In one sense there is only the prayer life of Christ, in which we ask some share, and yet our vocation leads us down avenues that may be proper to Franciscans.

St. Francis saw Christ as the great mediator between earth and heaven. Jesus remains the Father's perfect gift—indeed, the fullness of divine revelation given to earth, and in turn, the personal means of returning to the Father. The perfect following of Christ requires perfect imitation of that mediation, eminently by Mary the Mediatrix, but in a lesser degree by all other believers. So the Founder presents himself to the Order and world as a "secondary" mediator that emanates from the doctrine of the Communion of Saints. He tried to simplify religious life to the gospel essentials; he called the Rule the "marrow of the gospel," and felt that any "glosses" or commentaries were irrelevant. Thus, as often has been repeated, he made "religious life common property." The Founder does not sit in the chair of wisdom nor atop a pillar of inaccessibility, but elbows his way into the masses, laughing, chatting, and singing songs of humor and love.

Gone was the lock-step of monasticism and the special privileges accorded to abbots and superiors with respect to kitchen and living facilities. The leaders in the Franciscan movement were to live a life in common with the rank and file, owning no privileges. Fraternity and equality did not exempt the subjects from absolute obedience to the superior. Conversely, a monastic abbot could legislate any appropriate exemptions and regulations, but Franciscan local superiors were a "centralizing" force that bound all the friars to the *vita et forma minorum*. St. Bonaventure wrote that a superior was the servant in material things, but the master in spiritual matters, because he was supposed to know the group tasks best.

In time the ministers evolved into visitators who upheld the *forma minorum*, and the chapters evolved into administrative bodies. Such was the opinion of Cajetan Esser, O.F.M., but in some matters he seems to have projected what would become the life and rule of the Friars Minor in later centuries.

The Founder himself showed ambivalence in several matters. For example, he allowed the use of money to care for the sick in the *First Rule*, but forbade it in the *Rule of 1223*. Thus from considering money a "necessary evil," St. Francis considered it an "unnecessary good," a very Franciscan spiritual attitude towards the material world. Their own manual labor was to be the source of "income," provided there was no exchange of money, and they were allowed to keep the tools of their trade that they had brought to the community. The historian, Lazaro Iriarte, on page 26 of his *History*, wrote "the Divine Office was said corporately." Thus early on the Order was tied into the spiritual life of the universal Church.

St. Francis' spirituality seemed at times to be inconsistent and changeable, ambivalent and contradictory. When he wrote the beautiful letter to the friars regarding the Eucharist, he confessed his sinful inability to address such an august subject. He commands the friars to observe his counsels about the sacraments, but ends by imploring them to preserve his letter to the end of the world.

He made himself subject to others toward the end of his life, yet, remaining master and patriarch, continued to give orders. There was scarcely a precept of his Rules that he did not contravene himself. He was adamant in forbidding ownership, for example, yet he established claim and evidently some kind of ownership of mountain tops and caves and islands. They were removed from the dwellings of men, to be sure, but they were his own and passed into the permanent possession of his confriars. When the rest of Italy sweated out the summer and sustained the sirrocco, Francis escaped to cooler haunts and prayed. He begged his food when he was so inclined. Yet in the Rule he made "the table of the Lord" the last resort and exhorted the friars to whom the Lord gave the ability to work with industry.

St. Francis expected the friary cloister to be observed and wrote in his *Second Rule* that the brothers were not to enter the monasteries of nuns. Yet he freely invited and "entertained" Fra Jacopa (Giacoma di Settesoli) in his own friary. Similar stories derive from early footnotes to history. The chronicle of the early English friars indicates they were forbidden to have painted objects in their chapel. This was considered inconsistent with the lifestyle of poor men. But Francis had paintings of creation made for the antependium of the altar in the hermitage of Cesi di Terni.

Francis told his friars not to seek papal bulls of permission or dispensation, as for the Portiuncula. Yet he wanted his followers to preach Christ. After the disastrous first preaching tour of duty, he deliberately sought approval from Innocent III, and accepted the bulls of 1218 and 1220 from Honorius III to prelates that the brothers be received amicably, because their way of life had been approved by the Church. Did Francis reconsider his position? In his *Testament* he forbade the friars to ask the Roman Curia, directly or indirectly, for documents for churches or permission to preach.

Another, seemingly obvious dimension of Franciscan spirituality is interior and exterior joyfulness. That quality was part of a knight's code of chivalry. He saw joy as the unmistakable sign of the Lord's presence, and Satan cannot disadvantage anyone who is characterized by joy. On the other hand, a sad person is easily put down and divested. He was not embarrassed to play act, as when he scraped one stick with another as if playing a violin or lute. He thought gloom to be the height (or depth) of hypocrisy in a friar minor.

The strong statements and actions of the Founder regarding poverty is closely related to Franciscan prayer life. It was so anomalous that the Bishop of Assisi, Guido, a venal cleric, was the same bishop who covered the naked young man with his own cope. He was the most powerful lord in the valley and owned about half of the property in the commune. Many wealthy or noble persons donated lands, manors, or castles to the Church to make reparation for their worst crimes and sins, as murder and adultery. Popes confirmed the long list of holdings and threatened ecclesiastical penalties against those who would tamper with them. This in fact was Bishop Guido's title to judge the young Francis before his father. The time of Guido's administration, wrote Arnaldo Fortini, was full of litigations, libels, and arbitrations (page 255). Even the Holy See had to intervene to make peace. Guido would physically attack those whom he considered hostile, and was known to argue over funeral fees at the very caskets of the dead.

When one talks about the Order's prayer life, one must begin with matters liturgical. In fact, the Order has always prided itself on conformity with the Church's expectations. The very assumption of the Roman Divine Office throughout the Order and using it in all parts of the world assured its ultimate adoption throughout the Catholic world. Feasts as well as popular devotions entered Church life through the Franciscan Order. In recent times Church people have seen that the liturgy itself is one of the most important apostolates the hierarchical Church can share with the laity. The liturgy teaches, inspires, and motivates. St. Francis saw this importance, but confined himself to sweeping out churches, keeping the sacred vessels and linens clean, and the Eucharist reserved in "splendor" as far as possible (*Solutions to Questions* 2, 11, 15).

When he traveled, the founder would pause and make time to pray the Office at the proper times of the day. This attitude of reverence appears in St. Bonaventure's writing about the "community" or "conventualism," the friaries sufficiently large to provide special sermons and lectures, counseling and confessions, sung liturgies, and so forth. Drawing the laity into the riches of the Church's treasury was perhaps the chief benefit of the Conventual movement. Although St. Francis is the inspiration of the Order's prayer life, St. Bonaventure is its formulator. We can trace his thinking in his writing, The *Six Wings of the Seraphim*. Briefly stated, it was more important for Franciscans of all three Orders to be talking *to* God, than merely *about* him, however praiseworthy the preaching.

Francis modified the monastic tradition and simplified the Office for the friars who were clerics. At the same time Pope Innocent III was reforming the Divine Office. From the origins of the Benedictine Order the Office was prayed *in choro*, that is, in choir stalls with huge double-faced psalters being read from either side. But Franciscans historically prayed the Office *in communi*, that is, "together," but without all the monastic niceties of standing and bowing, turning to the altar, bowing to the hebdomadarian, and so forth, especially singing. This was more convenient to itinerant friars and preachers. Of course, the illiterate friars in the end were able to substitute the recitation of a series of Our Fathers. In addition, they were all to pray for the dead and for the failings of the friars. These regulations the Founder applied to the hermitages. We see a subtle monastic influence here. The Benedictine Rule states that the monastic tradition is designed to lead to the solitary eremitical life.

Because the Divine Office is regulated by the *ordo* or "order of prayer" of the whole Church, there is little room for distinctly Franciscan themes and directives. Besides, the Divine Office can so easily evolve into a ritualistic exercise, that spontaneity and personal investment readily disappear. The participants must remember the Office is primarily the prayer of Jesus Christ with whom we share the glory of praising God with the entire Church.

The Divine Office is centered on the Mass and Holy Eucharist. St. Francis' frequent references to the Eucharist and the priesthood are well known. We recall how one citizen of Rimini challenged St. Anthony to induce his starving mule to adore the Blessed Sacrament instead of eating. St. Clare overcame the attack of the Saracen mercenaries of Emperor Frederick II by showing the monstrance containing the consecrated Host at the window of San Damiano Monastery. Other Eucharistic miracles exist in Franciscan churches, as Siena and Lanciano. The point is that the Blessed Sacrament focuses our prayer life without our requiring a miracle to confirm it. For believers no confirmation is necessary; for unbelievers no confirmation is possible.

A second facet of Franciscan spirituality is the Marian dimension. Thomas Celano describes St. Francis' devotion to Mary, to whom he entrusted his Order, because "it was she who made the Lord of Majesty our brother." He poured out praises to her, composed prayers to her. He asked her to be the Order's advocate and protect the friars till the end of time.

It is another whole, wonderful story how in modern times, the Marian aspect of Franciscan spirituality has increased in manifold ways, particularly through the agency of St. Maximilian Kolbe, the martyr of charity of Auschwitz, and the international organization he founded, the Militia of the Immaculate.

The Eucharist and our Blessed Lady are not the only dimensions of Franciscan spirituality that derive from the Founder; for example, reading the book of creation, a concept from the Victorines, Richard and Hugh, developed by Bonaventure into exemplarism, or finding God's fingerprints and footprints as the relics of his creative acts. The theological facts are more complex with neo-Platonic theories and the triple way of purgation, illumination, and union.

An important series of biblical texts that describes the anointed of Yahweh, whether as an individual or the Chosen People. The liturgy applies Second Isaiah, chapters 42, 49, 50, and 53 during Holy Week to Christ, and there are abundant allusions to Second Isaiah in Matthew, Acts, and the Letters. Once more the Paschal Mystery is being played out, and it is eminently repeated in St. Francis' life: failure and death is predicted for the Lord's anointed, but his justification and glorification will surface only in his followers after his demise. Let us review briefly the texts of these Isaian Songs:

(42) The Chosen One has the spirit of God. He will not be an agitator, but a quiet voice, gently teaching justice. Yahweh forms him into a convenant for his people, to be their

light and freedom from darkness.

(49) He is Yahweh's sword and arrow. From the womb he was destined to bring back the Chosen People, and even the nations shall be saved. The one despised shall be honored by the earth's rulers.

(50) Yahweh trains his tongue and opens his ear to understand, although he is beaten and spat upon. Yahweh steels him to bear confrontation and defends him.

(52 and 53) Though he was disfigured the servant shall amaze the nations. Who could conceive such an unpresentable person, avoided because of his suffering and weakness? But he was crushed for our sins and by his wounds were we made whole. He was so silent under oppression that everyone thought his effectiveness was over. Yet his sufferings will help untold numbers and generate many descendants, while his own reward will be among the great.

One can, of course, easily predicate these texts of Francis. He was chosen by God as the remedy of his time. Filled with the Holy Spirit, his was a gentle voice, not stridently attacking corruption. His three Orders were a "covenant" people, for whom he was the principal light. His Order spread throughout all the nations and Francis himself was the "sword," the knight of the Lord's spiritual warfare by his preaching and listening to the Word. He was beaten by his father, by robbers, by suspicious believers, by the Muslims, and even rejected by some of his own confreres as leader, but his heart bore these and other confrontations. Francis was a "plain" man, not very presentable in appearance. By his setbacks we have come to understand ourselves better. By his stigmata we were assured that the Lord vindicated his charism. Now he is glorified by generations of Franciscans.

The Suffering Servant theme is prominent in all the saints' lives, but in St. Francis' biography the theme pervades his ministry and meaning to the Church, not only in his prayers and preaching, but also in the culmination in the stigmata on

Mt. Alverna. Closely linked is the ideal of the Scriptures as the formative principle of Franciscan spirituality. St. Francis called the Rule the "marrow of the gospel." He alludes to his favorite Bible texts throughout his writings. He lived in biblical awareness of the master plan of spiritual warfare and victory. He was rather literal, somewhat fundamentalist. This was long before the time of reliance on psychology and statistics, sociology and values clarification. Although there is only one spirituality, which derives from the Bible, the Second Vatican Council urged religious institutes to recover their specific charisms and relate them to the institutes' spiritual lives.

Although the Eucharist, our Lady, the Suffering Servant and the Bible are keys to Franciscan spirituality, there are other elements that appear, both natural and supernatural. There is Franciscan joy in God's benevolence towards mankind and the beauty of his creation. The Franciscan relationship is simple and spontaneous, down-to-earth and with few rules. The title of the Order, Friars Minor, bespeaks a tolerant humility, the "brotherhood of the lowly" or the "family of the unimportant." The affectivity characteristic of the Franciscan Order is centered on Christ, who models our relationship with one another and with our heavenly Father. Franciscan spirituality is a type of mysticism that cedes to practicality, a realism that is not rigid and avoids empty ritual.

CHAPTER X

Asceticism and the Joy of Friendship

Mortification is irrevocably bound up with the religious state in the eyes of most persons. Some religious assume that a rather consistent crossing of nature is a kind of price God exacts for grace. It is as if one should feel guilty in religious life for enjoying anything too much. Former Books of Customs for some institutes warn against such diverse "wickedness" as stroking a cat or celebrating a birthday—because it hearkens back to the days when we were "in the world." In the attempt to become detached from the beautiful and refined, some religious became attached instead to the ugly and, worse, to a smug self-concept of "holier-than-thou." A great deal of such mortification, unrelated to practical ministry, does more to destroy the psychic energy necessary for human growth than to retard any sin which is corrosive to human growth. The seven deadly sins derive from the same basic drives as creativity, play, rest, awareness of one's perfectibility, the imitation of ideal figures, physical fitness, and so forth. A better term is "basic instincts," rather than seven "deadly sins," or perhaps "basic thrusts of human nature."

Nevertheless, it seems spiritually dangerous to dismiss off-handedly what apparently nourished the mystical life of the Church for so many centuries. The first Eastern monks were hostile to the senses as if it were a terrible onus to have a body—which is not very sound theology. St. Benedict, on the other hand, prescribed a life style not unlike that of the Italian peasants as to food, garb, and rest. St. Francis, however, merely repeated the ascetical directives of the New Testament, which are usually very general applications of "the cross." The only concrete injunction he added was prescribed fasting in imitation of the Lord. The restrictions in garb merely echoed the Lord's command to his apostles about a second tunic. The Third Order Rule, which St. Francis did not himself write, required the same modesty in dress and social functions, but with more abstinence than the Church at large practiced. But even from this, members were excused if pregnant or traveling, and during bloodletting, and on holidays. When St. Francis heard at a Chapter that many brothers used hair shirts and metal devices to inflict pain on their bodies, he *forbade* these outright. Perhaps he feared that pride might result, or that physically exhausted brothers would be useless in the ministry, or that there was some psychological danger in keeping the physical aspect of transitory human existence so continually before the mind.

There was some development here in St. Francis' thought as he clarified his charism and related his life style to the gospel directives. In the *First Rule* he wrote, "The Spirit of the Lord wishes the flesh to be mortified and despised, and to be held of little value, lowly, and contemptible" (Chapter Seventeen). In Chapter Ten of the same Rule he tells the sick to

thank God, "for those predestined to eternal life are mortified by rods of suffering, weakness, and a spirit of sorrow, as
the Lord remarks, 'Whoever is dear to me I reprove and chas-
tise' " (Revelation 3:19). Yet St. Francis was equally solici-
tous in his Rules for the alleviation of the suffering of the
ailing brothers. If the "flesh" merely represented what was
hostile to the Spirit of God, even in this passage one would
have no quarrel with the Founder. In any case, the *Second
Rule*, which actually contains more concrete directives than
the prior writing, does not make such statements about the
vileness of the body.

If the Franciscan mandate is to reduplicate the gospel
life, one must turn to the pages of Scripture to see how the
Apostolic Age remembered the life of Christ and transmitted
its impressions to subsequent centuries. Jesus gave no ascetical
prescriptions outside the context of making the life of preaching and service more effective—no staff for the journey, taking up one's cross daily, giving one's goods to the poor so as
to be free of encumbrances on a tour of duty. Prescinding
from what St. Francis thought was useful asceticism for his
personal spiritual growth, we see that he legislated and taught
and permitted only what served the brothers' ministry. The
apostolic life was the rationale of asceticism. In his backward look at his life, the *Testament*, Francis observed that he
began to do penance and that what was bitter to nature became sweet on the occasion of his first *ministerial* act, which
was in imitation of Christ's frequent service—that is, St. Francis
began to nurse the lepers and even to kiss their limbs. Asceticism grows out of ministry, rather than the reverse—which
latter frankly appears to be the slant of religious formation
all too often; that is, if you keep stifling the demands of nature by an active program of physical and mental denial, God
will favor the assignment you are given. This is the "savings-
account" mentality—so much grace for so much mortification. Sin is a "debit" and fasting pays a "dividend."

In St. Francis' view, the mere absence of deliberate sin

and the self-control of mortification are pseudo-perfection. Misery is fruitless and asceticism is pointless except as a share in the mystery of Christ—that is, not so much the Christ of the Passion, as the Christ struggling with anxiety and tension from establishing his messianic position and extending God's kingdom all during his earthly sojourn. This is the ultimate, ministerial meaning of the tribute paid by St. Francis to the asceticism of Brother Ass before his death. "I give testimony that it has been in every way obedient, refusing nothing, but anxious to fulfill every command; Brother Ass neither avoided exhaustion nor escaped discomfort in order to achieve my demands" (Celano, *Second Life*).

In a sense it is not enough to probe only the New Testament in order to clarify the rationale of Franciscan asceticism. As a law-giver Christ was the second Moses, and as a voice of God, the last of the prophets. In himself he summed up the destiny of God's family; he relived its crucial moments of history. Like Moses, he spent forty days alone with God; like Israel, he wandered in the desert of temptation. In each instance God had to sustain and provide even the nourishment to keep his people alive and trusting in his fatherliness. Austerity was not so much chosen as imposed by the exigency of establishing God's kingdom in the Old and New Testaments. The anguish of Israel over Egyptian fleshpots and the temptation of Christ to yield to mere nature are a kind of suffering inescapably related to the extension of God's kingdom. Men are incapable of spiritual success until they depend on God. Israel must be chastised through human agents, as during the Exile, in the sense that self-dependence automatically removed Israel from God's care. Just as St. Paul was later to remark about God's choice of the foolish and weak, Zephaniah spoke of the "remnant" of the spiritually hungry and apparently powerless Israelites who were to continue God's family (cf. Zeph. 3:12-13). They were the *anawim*, the poor in spirit. (I am indebted in this section of the chapter to the writings of Barnabas M. Ahern,

C.P., particularly New Horizons, Notre Dame, Indiana: Fides, 1965).

Poverty of spirit in the religious institute or in lay life is more related to asceticism than to material poverty as we usually apply that first beatitude. Another translation of *anaw* is "meek"; so it is used to describe Moses in Chapter Twelve of Numbers as the meekest man on earth—one who was so unprepossessing that Aaron had to speak for him, yet a man utterly dependent on God in his personal anguish of soul. Mary, God's lowly and obscure handmaid, remarked in her Magnificat that God struck down the proud and mighty in the conceit of their hearts, while he tenderly looked after the cause of his *anawim*. Similarly St. Paul gloried in his weakness because the power of God thus became more obvious.

Suffering in its own right, therefore, originally had no meaning in Jewish and Christian thought. It cannot be isolated from the context of God's family being built up and finally perfected at the end of the world. So Isaiah, speaking in the person of Yahweh, tells Israel to keep a better fast and to do more appropriate penance than that of sackcloth and ashes to win his favor. Rather should they forego false claims, ease each others' burdens, and share their homes, clothes, and food with the needy (cf. Isaiah 58:4-9). Christ preached and practiced this kind of "penance" as a dimension of his apostolate also. Hence the risen Lord told his disciples on the way to Emmaus, "Did not the Messiah have to undergo all this so as to enter into his glory?" (Luke 24:26). The suffering of Christ culminated in crucifixion, but it was always present in his anxiety to fulfill his mission by preaching and in his compassion for those *anawim* whom he served. He himself was the supreme *anaw*, for in his ministry he had less than the foxes and birds; he had not whereon to lay his head. It was not merely the cross of Calvary that he carried; he denied himself and took up the cross of ministry daily. Asceticism in this case is not predicated on the depravity of man, but on his perfectibility and potential spiritual dignity. When

Christ tells his disappointed apostles, weary of an unsuccessful ministry, that some devils are cast out only by prayer with fasting, the matter is best understood as deprivation of rest, of visible success, and of feelings of satisfaction and exhilaration. The apostles are to go off alone to pray and fast in order to become *anawim*; they are men bereft of human consolation and fanfare, dependent on God alone to nourish them, isolated in their hearts, and deprived of human power in their ministry. It is God's friendship which supplies the empty places in the heart.

In both his Rule , therefore, St. Francis links fasting and that spirit of prayer to which all human endeavors must cede. He captures the mind of Christ in the *First Rule*, Chapter One, when he quotes Matthew 19:21 and 16:24; and Luke 14:26. Like the Master himself, our Founder delineates his charism by telling us that asceticism is a consequence of the gospel life more than a prior requisite. Three principles suggest themselves from the foregoing concepts. (1) The servant of Christ must reckon with the hostility of "the flesh"—which in St. Paul's writings means the burden of Adam's sinfulness, or the difficulty of responding to God's message of love. Such obstacles in himself and his clients lead the Christian to depend on God alone for effectiveness. (2) Those who aspire to the Franciscan charism, including secular tertiaries, must forego physical comforts, spiritual consolation, human fellowship, and so on, in a kind of self-denial appropriate to their state in life. (3) The degree of their dedicated love of God's family is assessed by their availability to those who need the word preached to them, and their accessibility to those who require healing, leadership, teaching, counseling, prayers, or whatever else the servant of God is able to provide. "Accessibility" is another name for "poverty."

Therefore, religious poverty is one expression of this asceticism. One must "risk" living by God's providence without storing up wealth and investments. If God inspires a new apostolate, he will provide the means; that is one way of determining whether a work is divine or merely human in origin. Another expression of this asceticism is celibacy, which frees the religious to love God's whole family. Virginity considered only as physical integrity in a man or woman is too narrow a definition. The celibate becomes an *anaw*, risking emotional desolation and hunger for acceptance of his ministry. The married Franciscan tertiary who understands his charism must take the same risks of not acquiring status symbols (poverty) and of losing the affection of his family (an extension of celibacy) in his exhorting others to do good (preaching) and in his hurrying to the aid of the disadvantaged (service). In this sense St. Francis made the religious or evangelical life common property of even the married.

It is even more important today than in St. Francis' time that we serve as a beacon of hope to man in his "existential frustration," as the saying goes. We must "suffer with," or have compassion. Sociology today tries to engineer human destiny. Studies and statistics are destroying man's individuality and creating some faceless "norm" or "median" as the typical standard around which we all gravitate. Behavioral sciences dictate the acceptable personality factors that often place the greatest stress on the very persons least able to acquire those factors. Therefore it seems that we are needed now more than ever before, to bring the divine friendship to earth.

St. Francis himself did not set up standards of acceptability. In his *First Rule* he said that even thieves are to be received in the friary. He must have remembered the occasion when he was driven away from a monastery because of his tattered appearance. Another time he changed the way of life of some brigands whom he served with courtesy and respect; a few of these men later entered the Order. St. Francis realized that hunger often reduced men to robbery in those days. He could call anyone "brother" and mean it, whether the person appeared evil, was rejected by others, or lacked the graces prized by worldlings.

This availability is learned in religious life (of all three Franciscan Orders) by bearing with the irritations and invasions of privacy within one's own religious family. This is not to say that putting up with drafts, leftover food, and headaches has no value—it has, particularly because these are mortifications of the passing moment, not chosen by ourselves. But the greatest value of these discomforts is to support and prepare the way for apostolic mortifications at the hands of rude or intrusive persons whose demands are unforeseen by us. In our own religious or blood-related families it is a ministerial act to listen to endless accounts of others' migraines, to lend a typewriter or umbrella when we are about to use it, or to accept the unsought advice of a would-be therapist. Just as the best training in sociology is to live among those with social problems, so the most important ministry to God's family is to one's own immediate family.

The title of this chapter links asceticism to joy. One's apostolate as a Franciscan must be casual and relaxed, since it ultimately depends on God for success. It must not be cluttered by too many rules of approach beyond kindly humor and brotherhood with fellow sinners. Struggle must coexist with laughter, and serious effort with being amused by one's own limitations. It is true that many individual acts of religious life must be performed with grim determination, or out of justice more than spontaneous charity. Acceptability to God does not depend on joy. But when joy is habitually absent, there is a real "credibility gap" for oneself as well as for the world regarding the value of this vocation.

No one skips through life with a perpetual smile of joy; no one's heart is light when he gets out of bed onto a cold floor early on a winter morning. But St. Francis reproved the dour visage and melancholy attitude. Only sin should make a brother sad. He called his brothers God's minstrels and *joculatores*, or "jokers." He even legislated joy in Chapter Seven of the *First Rule*: "The brothers should show themselves joyful and content in the Lord, merry, and becomingly courteous."

Joy is a part of that optimism which tells a man he will win the next race or the one after that. So at our profession ceremonies we are not covered by black palls prostrate on the floor with a funereal tolling of bells to announce our death to the world. Conscious, rather, of the total Paschal mystery, including the resurrection, we sing *Te Deum*, congratulate one another with a kiss of peace, sing our snappiest hymns. Then, delighted that we have been given to the world for its joyful salvation, we have a great party afterwards. That is how the friends of God habitually act.

St. Francis himself seemed to have alternated between elation and even manic activity and, conversely, depression and loneliness. His personal history was bizarre. He took off all his clothes in public to spite his father. He tried half a dozen careers at which he failed or didn't persevere. He feared contacts with women, even holy women. His adolescent fantasies about war and love were unreal. He thought learning was a possession of the mind, contrary to poverty. He made many saccharine statements, and talked with birds and animals, worms on the wet pavement, stray lambs, ferocious wolves, predatory bandits. He had outrageous expectations of others. There wasn't a vocation director who would have accepted him after the first interview.

Nevertheless, in his joy he taught the medieval world to celebrate whatever was born of the great womb of Mother Earth, even our Sister Death. Were he in our modern cities, he would hail "Brother Skyscraper," "Sister Micro-chip," and baptize politics and science and business, and accept rockets, neon signs, and computers as co-workers, inasmuch as this passing world will claim them, because in this post-Christian world what we do not celebrate *in* God and *for* God, we lose from the kingdom *of* God.

I think St. Francis came to know what his contemporaries did not because he recognized the human face of God in Jesus Christ, not by book learning, but by experience extrapolated to other human beings and nature itself. In Jesus Christ

God put a human face on his friendship and tenderness and also on his interest and involvement in our lives. At the Last Supper Jesus proclaimed that divine friendship, "I will no longer call you slaves, but friends, because I told you everything I heard from my Father." Further, he promises to send another Paraclete, the Spirit of joy and truth.

The divine friendship that is the source of joy might remain just another inane and moralistic generality except for its precision of meaning. Look at the nature of friendship. Friends encounter one another on the *basis of equality*. Otherwise the one begins to be manipulated or exploited by the superior or stronger. Friends share their *intimate secrets*. They dare even to risk rejection and ridicule when they reveal themselves. Friends *sacrifice themselves* by compromise, sharing, giving up, self-investment.

Now this is exactly what Jesus has done for us. (Compare with the above.) Jesus made himself our equal through the Incarnation. "He emptied himself out, did not cling to his divinity, but took the appearance of a servant. He was like us in all things but sin." Secondly, he shared his secrets— his nature, mercy, love—and the Paraclete continues as that other great revelation of divinity. Finally, Jesus sacrificed himself in his life and by his death. Jesus relates in friendship to all believers in this way. In our personal lives we enter the realm of friendship by imitating his human virtues, open ourselves to his graces, and sacrifice our lives and talents. The amazing awareness of friendship with God is the source of Franciscan spiritual joy.

St. Francis transferred his friendship (as I have explained it) to all the world, especially the poor to make them his equals in respect and hopefully standards of living. He shared his secrets with others, his surpassing knowledge of Jesus Christ, his love and mercy. Francis lived for his ministries and service, in keeping with the Franciscan charism, which is always suffused with joy.

In the spirit of joy we accuse no one, only ourselves for doing too little, for not respecting those who are different, for not joyfully treating this world as a gift. Like the founder we should be a *happy traveler*, hustling toward our dream of trying to change at least our corner of the world; a *tip-toe* person, poised to look with silent awe at creation and then a little farther to its maker; a *rememberer* of what Jesus said and did, and joyfully reflecting on his message to us; a *fringe* person, preferring to live at the edge of society and by choosing the *marginated* as special friends (as analyzed before), the lepers, poor, and outcasts; and the *threshold* person, waiting in the antechamber of heaven for the promise of eternal life.

The purpose of joy and asceticism and of every virtue, we must remember, is the following of Christ, conformity to his earthly existence. The Spirit leads us to concretize that conformity in activities and apostolates. No wonder St. Francis was at times bewildered; the Order seemed shapeless and unpredictable, growing almost cancerously in every direction. He finally had to let go of even the Order he founded and live tentatively as he personally underwent his own process of individuation and brought redemptive value to the mystery of salvation within the Order. Is there anything greater a Founder can do? In the *Rule of 1221* he wrote, "Our friends are those who for no reason cause us trouble and suffering, shame or injury, pain or torture, even martyrdom and death. It is these we must love and love very much, because for all they do for us, we are given eternal life" (Chapter 22).

The cross of Jesus was a lifelong preoccupation of Francis. He composed a not very original Office of the Passion, which consists mostly of Psalms, Bible passages, and a few phrases of the saint himself. The Office was arranged for five seasons of the year, beginning with Holy Week. Thus Francis made room for the Crucified in his life. To be emptied out of one's vanity and foolish ambition is the spiritual work of every man. To make room for another is the proper activity of a believer. Thus the Master is, as it was predicted by Simeon at his presentation, *the ultimate sign of contradiction to be imitated by Francis*: one is free only when he gives himself to another in complete love; one is a true lover only when he risks unendingly without expecting recompense.

Kenosis is not a complex spiritual process, just a slow and painful one. There is *first of all* the self-imposed emptying—under the influence of grace, of course, but controlled and willed by oneself. Such is the assumption of penance, the life of vows, a humble life style, true asceticism, the service of others, risking pain and discomfort, and so forth. The *other kind of kenosis* is accepted, but not controlled. Such is one's environment of heat and cold, body sickness and fatigue, betrayal and mockery and disillusionment, temptations of all kinds, and so on. Simultaneously the "purgation" of the person and his "illumination" are taking place. But it is generally a more significant *mortification* (which means "death-dealing") to endure the *second kenosis*: what derives from our state in life, our role in community or family, and our job assignment.

We see in Francis' life how he developed from the first to the second emptying. We, too, learn in *kenosis* to *surrender immediate gratification* for the sake of long-range goals. It is human to expect instant feedback, affirmation, and positive strokes. It is gratifying to hope for a little applause from those we serve, if only to reassure ourselves in our life roles. Yet many tasks, whether teaching or administration or raising a family, may require a wait of even years to see the effectiveness of our work. Meanwhile we enter God's presence as beggars and offer what we have: *the sacramentality of our lives,* that is, the invisible grace which permeates mundane activities to give ordinary work its spiritual meaning. Our concomitant prayer makes us part of the Church's rhythm of life, even when it is unrewarding, dry, a burden. *Our moral presence to others* then goes beyond mere "parallel living," which of itself does not foster the believing community. Moral presence is often a keen *kenosis*-including concern, involvement, and sacrifice when we are "hurting" ourselves. The length of time we spend with others is less important than the intensity and availability and quality of presence we demonstrate. We soon learn the close correlation there is between our ability to love God, whom we do not see, and our ability to love our neighbor, whom we do see. *We become less inclined to assert our "rights,"* even to a good name, but use this world, which is fast passing away, with care, respect, and restraint. Most of all, we try to *get out of God's way.* Our hardest efforts are seldom the cause of our signal successes. "It is God who gives the increase," and to him belongs the glory. We finally *let go of personal projects* and *preconceived ideas* (even of our spiritual lives) and let God fill the void, which is the only way I know of becoming "perfect as your heavenly Father is perfect." And this is done in the joy of friendship with God, perfection has reached its summit.

CHAPTER XI

The Poor in Spirit

Each of the vows somehow presupposes the other two and makes them operative. Chastity frees a Franciscan for many kinds of ministry through obedience. Obedience creates the environment to observe the structures of poverty. Poverty in a sense encompasses most of the virtues of the spiritual life, because it requires the dispossession of self. Poverty teaches respect for life and beauty and the goodness of God's creation. Religious attempt to disencumber themselves more radically by open profession of the liberating gospel—the vow of poverty (freedom from materialism), chastity (freedom from erotic demands), and obedience (freedom from arrogance and tyranny over others). Of course, all Christians revere these three vows, at least as "counsels" given in the gospel, or "pieces of advice."

How the vows are interpreted depends on one's charism and that of the community. By "charism" I mean that gift of

the Spirit made to an individual or group as its chief beneficiaries, but intended to build up the whole Church as a new
creation, helping individuals to become a child of God with a
new spirit. "All who are led by the Spirit of God are sons of
God. You did not receive a Spirit of slavery leading you back
into fear, but a Spirit of adoption through which we cry out,
'Abba!' (that is, 'Father'). The Spirit himself gives witness
with our Spirit that we are children of God." (Romans 8:14-
16).

Who knows how many tons of paper have been covered
with zealous and sometimes fanatical writing about the subject of Francis' essential charism? It may have been joy, his
prayer life, fixation on Jesus' passion, charity, apostolic preaching, emotionality. Sometimes non-essential elements or events
of Francis' life may have conditioned the statement of charism,
as Francis' flair for drama and "acting out"—for example,
preaching to birds when men did not listen, putting worms
off the roadway so his crawly brothers might not be trampled,
or taking off his habit so he might lie naked in death. Yet
charism must exclude novelties, transitory actions, and idiosyncratic gestures, as challenging Moslem holy men to a trial
by the ordeal of fire.

The terms of the Order's title, "friar" and "minor," are
often linked as the expression of his charism. These are
important Franciscan concepts, although scarecely new in
Francis' time. There were those who called themselves
"brothers" living the common life, as well as "minors," who
were disenfranchised or the "less important" members of
society (Cf. Mockler, page 176). Although the distinction
between *maiores* and *minores* was not a common political
division, this distinction was used in the *Carta Pacis*, No-
vember 9, 1210, when Francis was in Assisi, and which ended
the class war by order of Emperor Otto. The concept undoubtedly appealed to Francis in his subsequent thinking.
Note, however, that both "friar" and "minor" bespeak a
kind of poverty, which is the subject of this chapter. It is the

very democracy in the Church that is a clarion call to poverty.

Francis combined the two terms into one title not so much as the statement of his charism (a word he did not use nor probably would have understood), but rather as the *human dimension* and *relationship* between those who followed him. They were to act as members of one family and identify with the lowly and simple and dispossessed. "Friar Minor" is sometimes translated as "Lesser Brother," but I prefer the "Family of the Unimportant"—which applies equally well to all three Orders.

Fraternity implies our surrender of excessive ego and individuation in order to serve the needs of the believing community. *Minority* implies our identification with the weak and our avoidance of personal power. "Fraternity " refers to interior change; "minority " refers to exterior change and implies our identification with the weak and avoidance of power.

To learn what it means to be a Franciscan and to learn the essence of Francis' experience is analogous to studying wildlife, in fact, some elusive animal always on the verge of extinction as an endangered species. (That is why we must constantly undergo conversion and reformation, to escape extinction!) There are three possibilities of research, each of which has its value. You can track an animal in the wild, live alongside it, film it, implant "beepers" in its neck. Analogously this is like living the Franciscan life directly as a matter of one's own experience. Secondly, you can study a species in a zoo, comfortably, but a little artificially, and observe its eating, mating, and bonding. This is analogous with discussing the Franciscan life with those who are already successful in somehow replicating the charism of Francis. Thirdly, you can achieve a certain closeness by viewing an animal through a taxidermist's skill in the museum of natural history—and yet be in one sense the farthest from the living truth. This last is analogous with reading about the Franciscan life and its

Founder. No doubt all three methods are required to have a full knowledge of the subject! And no doubt this is clearer about poverty than the other vows, life style, and ministries of St. Francis of Assisi. During the century preceding Francis there was considerable dissatisfaction with the clergy and religious of the day, especially regarding poverty. New forms began to emerge. Nicholas II in 1059 remarked that the common life was a feature of the life of the apostles, and Rupert of Deutz had to defend traditional monasticism against the popularity of the canons regular flourishing then by asserting that the apostles were just like the monks of his day. Stephen of Thiers-Muret claimed that the only true source of religious life was the Gospel. Next, also in the century before Francis, Vitalis of Savigny became an itinerant preacher and social worker in order to live the life of the apostles. The founder of the Premonstratensians, Norbert of Gennep, gave away his money, went about barefoot to preach, and tried to reconcile warring factions. He told his followers to use this greeting: Peace be to this house. Obviously he was much like Francis in all these matters. Most of these movements consisted of laypersons; the important aspect was that religious lifestyle was no longer confined to cloisters.

One religious congregation, the Humiliati, even developed its own Third Order by 1201. Poverty became the hallmark of most of these groups; Innocent III even gave the title of "Poor Catholics" to one group. Like Francis soon to come after them, they called each other *fratres*, followed the counsels as commands, recited the *Paternosters*, and fasted on the days prescribed by the Church only. They promised to obey the Pope and the clergy. All this has been written about clearly and succinctly by Fr. Duane Lapsanski, OFM, in his dissertation, "Evangelical Perfection." He points out on page 50, "It is evident, therefore, that when Francis of Assisi and his companions came to Rome in the year 1210 (09) to obtain the Church's blessing and approval for their form of life, neither their outward poverty, nor their basic desire to live the gospel was anything radically new.   Rather, Francis' vision was the highpoint and the summation of Christian values which had inspired the hearts of zealous persons for more than a century and a half."

An important question that plagues the historian is why Francis succeeded with poverty when these others failed to continue within the Church. Of course, God's will is the final answer. But humanly speaking, we can see the forces of history at work. The time was not ripe for Francis; others had to prepare the way. The hierarchy, including the Pope, had not yet become alarmed at the incipient heresies, against which the new religious Orders would be a buffer. Finally, the identification of Francis with Jesus was so complete and his humanity so obvious and his joy so contagious, that the future of his Order was assured by the natural as well as the supernatural forces behind it.

Right at the beginning of the *Rule of 1221* Francis wrote, "The *Rule* and life of the friars is to live in obedience, in chastity, and without property, following the teaching and the footsteps of our Lord Jesus Christ..." At the beginning of the final *Rule of 1223* Francis wrote, "The Rule and life of the Friars Minor is this, to observe the holy Gospel of our Lord Jesus Christ by living in obedience, without anything of their own, and in chastity." In the *Testament*, the third of his most important documents, he wrote, "When God gave me a few brothers, there was no one to tell me what to do, but the Most High himself instructed me to live the life of the Gospel." The idea of the Gospel life is found in Francis' *Memorandum to Clare*: "It was God who inspired you to become the daughters and servants of the Most High supreme King and Father of heaven, and to espouse yourselves to the Holy Spirit by choosing to live according to the perfection of the holy Gospel..." The newness of Francis' way of life is emphasized in Brother Elias' letter to all the friars announcing Francis' death. Celano emphasizes this point by calling Francis the new evangelist, or "Gospel writer." A very important statement by Celano is that Francis recovered the life of the primitive Church, which appears both in the *Vita Secunda* and *Tractaus de Miraculis*.

The *Sacrum Commercium cum Domina Paupertate* by an unknown Franciscan is a medieval dialogue or skit with the friars coming to visit and serve their Lady, Poverty. She says in one passage, "The Apostles rejoice to see their own life renewed." Similarly the *Tres Socii*, responding to a General Chapter mandate to write their recollections about 1246, wrote that the vocation of Francis was to live according to the form of the holy Gospel; and that the friars preached this Gospel, holding all things common. The same ideas: observing the Gospel, following the footsteps of Jesus, and recovery of the apostolic community, are found in official documents and the liturgical texts. Duane V. Lapsanski, O. F. M, (*Evangelical Perfection*, St. Bonaventure, New York: The Franciscan Institute, 1977) presents the viewpoints of two important persons more in detail. Hugh of Digne was a friar from Provence. He thought that Francis was unique in not choosing just some of the gospel injunctions for his followers, but the gospel in its totality, not as an abstract ideal, but as a living reality.

Jacques de Vitry is important as an outsider viewing the new Order. He explains that the Order grew so rapidly because it imitated the way of the primitive Church and of the apostles, drawing out pure waters from the evangelical fountain. They fulfilled not only the precepts, but even the counsels of the Gospel and followed the naked Christ. Being like the primitive Church meant to have one mind and heart, as the first Christians in the Acts of the Apostles.

Ewert Cousins wrote that in the *Legenda Minor* Bonaventure "was to characterize the virtues of the Poverello as so many ways in which he was made like to Christ" (page XV). Cousins wrote in the same work, "Bonaventure is proposing (Francis) to the friars and to Christians in general as a model of the gospel way of life... Although he is a new prophet and an angelic spirit, he is first and foremost an imitator of

Christ." (page 45) Bonaventure himself wrote in the *Epistola de tribus questionibus* about his own Franciscan vocation, "I acknowledge before God that what made me love the life of blessed Francis so much was the fact that it resembled the beginning and growth of the Church. As the Church began with simple fishermen and afterward developed to include renowned and skilled doctors, so you will see it to be the case in the Order of blessed Francis. In this way God shows that it was not founded by the prudence of men but by Christ."

In some ways this likeness to the early Church was a mixed blessing. One should not "canonize" all the early Christians any more than all the early friars!

In a quick overview we see that the view of essential Franciscan life as the pure and simple Gospel, which developed certain accretions and restrictions in the hands of some early commentators. Mention of "ascetical practices" began to liken the fraternity to existing Orders of monks. "Observance without gloss of the Rule" or the requirement to observe only "Gospel precepts" developed into a spirit of legalism. Emphasis on the "missionary discourse" and a heavy accent on priest-friars over brother-friars after the IV Lateran Council, when more priests entered the Order and its members were required by the Holy See to study. Interestingly neither "friar" nor "minor" figures prominently at that time in the delineation of the Franciscan charism. The watering down of the full Gospel inspiration occurred not only during Francis' lifetime, but equally during the days of the primitive Church. We know this not only from the Letters of Paul to the Church at Corinth and the altercations that figure in the *Acts of the Apostles*, but from the accounts of heresies and backsliding from other sources, especially the first Fathers of the Church. History gives evidence of the clericalization of the Church (so the laity lost its ministries), a "comfortable" asceticism, the growing legalism, even pharisaeism, much like the Franciscan Order! This is not say that laxity was the order of the day; in fact, in *their* weakest and most lax moments they may have far exceeded *our* attempts, especially in the practice of poverty today.

When you join the Franciscan Order, even the Third Order, that society has certain "given's," as about poverty and existing commitments. "Filling slots" is not necessarily evil; in fact, it may be the primary expression of poverty in our times. Not only are we humans prone to judge others, but the very nature of our psyches requires constant evaluations and critiques of our environment. As in so many aspects of poverty seen in this subtle understanding of dying to self, the most important action of poverty is getting out of the way of God! That is why it is appropriate to say that this vow affects the other two and, indeed, the religious life of all Franciscans.

Of all the written works about how St. Francis conformed to Christ, the most thorough was undoubtedly the *Book of Conformities* written by Bartholomew of Pisa several centuries ago. Absolutely unscholarly, totally mystical and decidedly poetic, the *Book of Conformities between the Life of Blessed Francis and the Life of the Lord Jesus* was considered by Paul Sabatier as the most important work ever written about the Founder. For many centuries every biography of Francis was, in a sense, the *Book of Conformities* updated and revisited. Although the volumes are seldom read now and have not ostensibly been translated into modern languages, their influence was widespread.

Among the familiar titles of the Founder have been the "Christ of Umbria," a "second Christ," the "living Gospel." When the Lord revealed himself to St. Margaret-Mary Alacoque, he gave her St. Francis as a model, because he was, more than anyone before him, like Christ. Yet in most of the events of the lives of both Jesus and Francis that can be determined, they had widely divergent personal histories. Christ was undoubtedly closely attached to his parents. He came from a much poorer family than Francis (although it may be justly said that Joseph the artisan belonged to the middle class).

Jesus did not pass through a variety of careers, and his "failure" and rejection were of the essence of his mission on earth. Jesus had no sibling rivalry, as Francis did, with his brother (or brothers). One can adduce many more dissimilarities.

But it is the likenesses we are after, particularly the *kenosis*, or the emptying out of poverty by Bartholomew of Pisa, (Bartholomaeus de Rinonico de Pisis). Two other Bartholomews have been mistaken for and merged with this author. For a short but thorough analysis of this author and his work, read Carolly Erickson, "Bartholomew of Pisa, Francis Exalted": *De Conformitate*. (*Medieval Studies*, Volume XXXV, 1972. Toronto: The Pontifical Institute of Medieval Studies. Pages 253-274).

He begins already in the Second Prologue, section 1, Vol. IV of the *Analecta Francescana*, pages 4 and 5, describing Francis' following of Jesus

"ad vivificandum... intuendum...delectandum... contemplandum... informandum... fortificandum... liberandum...recreandum...   refocillandum... venerandum...   imitandum...   exoptandum... quietandum... indulgendum et condonandum... purgandum peccata et extergendum... gubernandum... prosternendum et superandum... perpetuandum... iubilandum... beatificandum... retribuendum... exprimendum et declarandum... sanandum... placandum... refrigerandum... adoptandum... anhelandum... redolendum... degustandum... intrandum...   serenandum...   irradiandum... reconciliandum... satisfaciendum... impetrandum... attestandum... peragrandum..."

These gerunds, of course, do not translate with the same effect! Such ploys appear throughout Bartholomew's work. The parade example is the *principium arbori*, the "metaphor of the tree," which is a kind of table of contents or framework of the treatise at its beginning, page 16 of the Second

Prologue. Couplets of Jesus' "fruits" rhyme, and so do the correlating Francis' "fruits"; unfortunately, the verses do not rhyme in translation:

Jesus parvus insignitur; Franciscus agitatur:

Jesus abiectus cernitur; Franciscus separatur;

Jesus hosti exponitur; Franciscus molestatur:

Jesus coetus prosequitur; Franciscus fecundatur.

Jesus legem dat populis; Franciscus regulator:

Jesus doctor mirabilis; Franciscus praedicator;

Jesus mandans discipulis; Franciscus destinator:

Jesus loquens humillimis; Franciscus reserator.

Etc., etc.

A case for these likenesses is made in a lengthy treatise that runs to two full volumes of small print in the Quaracchi Edition of the *Analecta Franciscana*, Volumes IV and V, published in 1906 and 1912.

The work of Bartholomew is excessive and illogical and tedious and totally delightful! He shows a masterful knowledge of both Testaments of the Bible; one wonders whether he had a concordance at hand. He quotes from mythology and profane history and whatever else he could get his hands on regarding the Franciscan Order, particularly the prophecies of Joachim of Flora. Bartholomew took forty aspects of Jesus' life and followed them piecemeal by forty comparisons aggregated from the words and biographies and legends of Francis. Along the way Bartholomew finds reasons to include most major Catholic doctrines, the problems within the Order (he sided with the authorities of the "community"), and lists of friaries and saints and notables—a veritable Franciscan encyclopedia of great value to historians.

His general framework was a tree with forty double-fruit-bearing branches—the "conformities"—yet after the initial statement the metaphor ceases to have relevance or even interest. Bartholomew shows medieval partiality to rhyming and assonantal lists of words, perhaps as a mnemonic aid. It may be helpful to provide a "sampler" here of Bartholomew's opus.

He plays the "numbers game"—three's and seven's are always most popular, being "mystical"—due to the general medieval attitude and Pythagorean influences on Augustine and Bonaventure, his mentors. He likes balanced antithetical phrases and figures of speech "curtseying" back and forth down the page if only to show that, after all, according to Franciscan logic, the whole of creation is but a metaphor of God.

Under "Francis is declared," that is, "foretold" in the Old Testament as Jesus himself, Francis is compared in sixty-four texts. For example, his rebuilding of San Damiano, San Pietro, and Portiuncula is compared to the work of Bezalel and Oholiab, who built the Lord's tabernacle in Exodus (38:22-23) and the work of Solomon, builder of the Temple in Kings (1:5ff). (Fruit one, second part, section 3). Comparisons limp very often, however. In Fruit three, second part, Bartholomew shows how the universe rejoiced at the physical birth of Jesus. The "conformity" is the joy of the world at the spiritual birth of Francis and his Order. Under Fruit six, first part, section 3, after describing Jesus' "abjection" by being lost as a boy in the Temple and forced to beg for his sustenance, Bartholomew has a long digression on the great personages of history who were brought low, first the men, then the women. The author is fairly lurid in his account—decidedly adult reading.

The title of Fruit eight is "A crowd follows Jesus," that is, the apostles. The "conformity" is "Francis is prolific." Bartholomew goes through the entire three Orders by provinces and lists their saintly persons since their inceptions, as well as the popes and cardinals. This occupies pages 178-364 of Volume IV of the *Analecta*. A scholion appears on pages 214-233, the "Sayings of Brother Giles." Under Fruit nine, second part, Bartholomew places an exposition of the *Rule of*

1223, taking up pages 370-457 of Volume IV. Scriptural passages are accumulated for each chapter, followed by a commentary, to which a defense of the life of the friars is added, laced with papal documents besides. The point is to "conform" Francis as *Regulator*, "giver of rules," with Jesus the Lawgiver. Much of the exposition is irrelevant and pietistic, but historically invaluable—providing much fuel for doctoral dissertations. Under Fruit eleven, "Jesus commissions his disciples," Francis is the "Sender." Bartholomew lists the current "places" or establishments and friaries of the Order according to provinces and divided into custodies and vicariates. This occupies pages 503-558 of Volume IV in small print. He mentions the famous and holy persons entombed in the friary churches. Fruit twelve is "Jesus addresses the lowliest," Francis is named *Reserator,* or the "revealer." Forty sermonettes appear, taken from the writings of and legends about Francis, pages 595-632 of Volume IV. For all these reasons Bartholomew's work is called the Franciscan encyclopedia. Yet it is seldom read or understood.

Volume V of the *Analecta Francescana* is more helpful regarding *kenosis.* Fruit sixteen is "Jesus is without resources and sparing," and Francis is "disfigured" or "dishonored." The treatment concerns evangelical poverty. Francis was generous to the poor when he was still "in the world" and associated with the deprived. He renounced worldly riches and then sought alms from door to door. Finally, he assumed Gospel poverty after listening to Matthew 10. He professed poverty, recommended it as the queen of virtues, and asked God to give him the grace to assume it. He wore cheap and patched clothes and allowed only poor dwellings to his followers, etc. (Pages 100-105 of Volume V). Fruit nineteen describes the austerity of Jesus and Francis, but not in terms of *kenosis.* (Pages 189-198) Fruit thirty-two is "Jesus fading from life" and "Francis is called forth." The rather brief passage regarding Francis describes the similarities between his death and that of Jesus (Pages 432-433).

The most valuable text of Bartholomew, who was first among hagiographers to attempt such a book of "conformities," appears in Volume V, pages 129-145. The twofold title is "Jesus submits to all" and "Francis is *made less*," from *minoratur*, a play on the name of the Order. Humility is the theme, and Bartholomew makes it Fruit seventeen. He cites eleven qualities of Francis one could rightly term *kenotic* in our present sense of poverty.

1. Love of humble and abject persons, especially the poor and lepers.

2. Joyful acceptance of injuries.

3. Shrinking from hearing himself praised.

4. Personal declaration of worthlessness.

5. Flight from high station.

6. Prompt submission to everyone.

7. Heartfelt embrace of humility.

8. Adaptation to others.

9. Denial of his own will and leading others to do the same.

10. Observance of God's precepts and counsels.

11. Meek and gentle lifestyle.

The topics related to *kenosis* are the following:

1. Self-professed lowliness of Francis.

2. Breaks with his family and class-consciousness.

3. Identification with marginal persons.

4. Letting go of friends and romantic notions and his own administration.

5. Acceptance of illness and weakness.

6. The living death of the Stigmata and his Sister Death.

Note how these topics relate to the poverty of being "emptied out," or *kenosis*.

Enough has been said of Bartholomew's monumental

work, which may well be interpreted as containing the themes and issues of poverty and "emptying out." Let us proceed further with the subtle gospel directive of poverty....

This elusive poverty of "being" takes its start from a sense of *creatureliness*. This is how we begin to "be perfect as your heavenly Father is perfect." He is the All-holy, the Totally Other than ourselves. It is not a question of calling oneself a "worm"—however true that may be at times because of sin. Our awareness of creaturehood or contingency and irrelevance and transitoriness leads us to be emptied of ourselves to make room for God. Because God is himself intangible, we pattern ourselves after his incarnate Son so we can be filled with something, or rather Someone. The second strophe of the *Canticle of Brother Sun* proclaims, "No mortal lips are worthy/To pronounce your name."

The beginnings of both extant Rules declare that the Rule and life of the friars is to live in obedience, in chastity, and with nothing of one's own (*sine proprio*). This poverty exceeds mere physical circumstances; it requires the expropriation of one's self-direction, self-concept, self-centering. The same initially negative concept inheres in the three Gospel texts that were surely written by Francis (not Caesar of Speyer) in the *Rule of 122*. "Go, sell what you have and give it to the poor" (Matthew 19:21.) "If anyone wishes to come after me, let him deny himself and take up his cross and come, follow me" (Matthew 16:24). "If anyone comes to me without turning his back on his father and mother, and wife and children, and brothers and sisters, yes and even his very self, he cannot be my follower" (Luke 14:26). This is being emptied of wealth, free will, family, relationships, and love of one's own life!

When Francis wrote the Hymn of Praises for Brother Leo, he poured out his adoration of the Most High. "You are strong, great, good, love, wisdom, humility, rest, strength, sweetness, etc." What does the saint imply except that he is weak, little, bad, hateful, stupid, proud, without peace, weak and bitter by comparison?

"We must be firmly convinced that we have nothing of our own, except our vices and sins. And so we should be glad when we 'fall into various trials' (James 1:2), and when we suffer anguish of soul or body, or affliction of any kind in this world, for the sake of life eternal." "We must hate our lower nature with its vices and sins...By our own fault we are corrupt, wretched, strangers to all good, willing and eager only to do evil." When a saint writes in this manner long after his conversion and maturation in holiness, it might be rash to criticize this self-deprecation simply because it is foreign to our times. Not only should virtue and vice be judged according to their proper century, but it is impossible to predict whether our own century's contrasting "self-fulfillment" will be judged as a corporate and massive ego-trip.

In his *Letter to a General Chapter*, probably before the Pentecost Chapter of 1224, or just two and a half years before he died, Francis confessed, "I have sinned in many ways, through my own most grievous fault, and in particular by not keeping the Rule which I promised to God, and by not saying the Office, as the Rule prescribes, through carelessness or sickness, or because I am ignorant and never studied." This mental set was not a beginner's attitude appropriate to the inception of the "purgative way" alone, but rather a lifelong concept appropriate to *kenosis*. It was not enough that Francis was graced by God with a sense of his creatureliness. He had to be uprooted from the value system of the City of Man and replanted in the soil of the City of God.

There is a tendency for religious of our time to isolate certain factors in the life of poverty and make these factors the total definition of poverty. This vow is now variously called one of "detachment," of "economy," of "dependence," or of "permission." It may be that such a factor is the totality of poverty for some religious institutes; especially if their life

style depends on large holdings of land or expanding investments; each institute must clarify its own charism. In any
case, detachment and permission do not excuse one from asking himself whether the possession or project being sought at
a particular moment is really compatible with one's type of
poverty in the first place.

Nevertheless, all the factors named above are typical of
any poor person who has little of his own. Once more, however, in the case of religious the absence of individual ownership could still allow considerable ease, even indulgence, under collective ownership. Each institute's charism, however,
must serve to make Christ present to the Church and to the
world, and every true gift of the Spirit must build up and
receive the approval of the body politic. In the spirit of continuing reformation, meaningless types of poverty must cede
to the significant. We already proposed the principle that the
vow of poverty is primarily a type of *asceticism that is conse-
quent upon the ministry* of preaching and service—at least in
our three Orders. Further, the factors of secularity and mobility condition the life style of a Franciscan. It may be useful, therefore, before specifically treating St. Francis' legislation and exhortation, to consider some general notions of
poverty as understood by the Catholic and non-Catholic
world, to whom we are sent as a sign of the Apostolic Age
come alive.

We may well wonder, if we ever achieve the "great society" without poverty, whether in such an environment we as
religious can live in relevance without possessions. (What
would some religious do nowadays without an "inner city"?)
Would such a nation or world look upon us as anything but
relics of the past, were we to live, cashless and comfortless, in
this theoretical land where there was abundance for all? Would
we have to redefine "poor" people merely as those lacking in
spiritual wealth? Analogously, if teaching, healing, and other
institutional services became so technical and diversified that
the religious institute could not provide adequate training any

more, would the service aspect of Christian ministry fall into desuetude?

Apart from this "paradise" existing only in the speculative imagination at present, other expressions of poverty (and service) would evolve, we can be sure, from reflection on the Gospel, just as modern social principles have been drawn by Christian thinkers from the pages of Scripture. The personality of an Order, as it was defined earlier, bespeaks potentials not yet arrived at. At all times the Gospel life of an available and mobile ministry would be the criterion of poverty. This refers not so much to what you *use*, but rather to how much you allow yourself to *be used*. Those whom we serve are more interested in the "psychological" austerity and self-denial mentioned in the last chapter than in the lack of material appurtenances in life. Once more, we not only serve God's *anawim*, but must become *anawim* ourselves in the sense that we *accept the conditions and clientele of the ministry* that God provides, rather than set up somewhat arbitrary levels of possession and use of material goods as absolute norms. We remember that the Man who had not whereon to lay his head during his mission frequently stayed with Lazarus, Mary, and Martha and enjoyed the refinements of an apparently wealthy home. And one can be sure that Mary, the mother of Jesus, as well as other friends, provided what comforts they could while the Lord was on the road. All this is written not to disparage traditional religious poverty, but to put it into proper context. Christ (and here is the point) was as satisfied with poor as with comfortable accommodations. In the very important enumeration of the beatitudes, the lowly, miserable, and deprived, the *anawim, are* identified more by spiritual than by material factors.

The best testimonial to poverty in an institute would be the coexistence—without jealousy or complaint—of many levels of poverty according to the kinds of ministry. If optimism and freedom of expression are a genuine legacy of St. Francis, this should be possible. In any case, it is dangerous to establish uniform regulations for "possession and use"; it is a fetish of a falsely democratic society. If a certain amount of "cash and comfort" becomes an inalienable right, members develop an attitude that they should by all means use up all they are entitled to. They soon forget that they become *anawim* by reducing their needs.

Poverty has always been such a characteristic of the Order that some Franciscans would make it the primary mark of our life. As a matter of fact, centuries ago Pope John XXII declared it a theological error that evangelical poverty was the highest form of imitation of Christ. Love of our heavenly Father, charity for our neighbor, apostolic availability, obedience to any life style the Spirit designs for us—such virtues supersede poverty in living the Christ-life. Just as it is false spirituality to assume that the vow of celibacy denigrates sex or human passion or the body of a person, it is equally out of step with the Scripture to conclude that the material advantages of this earth are evil. Hence poverty is not the same as tasteless living quarters, clothes, and food. Beauty and practicality are more Christian than their opposites. Whatever threatens the mental well-being of the apostle or disciple of Christ with respect to possessing either too much or too little is the wrong kind of poverty for him. One's ego is so involved, and properly so, with satisfaction in his ministry, that each person must consider himself in the double role of a Christ-figure and a professional person. The individual conscience is the final forum: like Christ, the Franciscan must be uncluttered by the *impedimenta* of living; as a professional, he must use the secular world's techniques. We read nowhere in the New Testament that Christ deliberately imposed any form of poverty on himself outside the context of the ministry. Some exegetes think that he even belonged to the middle rather than the lower class of Jews. He once rebuked Judas' false concern for the poor by remarking that they are always with us and lauding the use of a valuable perfume on his body. He told no one merely to dispossess himself, but to give one's possessions away as a part of entering the ministry alongside him. Dispossession forced a person to become *anaw*, that is, dependent on God and inspired benefactors for support.

It is specious, therefore, to reason that large and efficient plants, such as hospitals, printeries, or schools, make witness to poverty impossible. In some cases, because of government subsidy or required standards of excellence, large operations are necessary. In this case, poverty consists of serving a poorer clientele and of expecting a modest fee—or none, if this can possibly be arranged. It is likewise specious to compare the social service of religious with the Peace Corps or governmental agencies. (We can readily see that the motivation of the latter is typically as noble as that of religious.) But social servants, after all, are paid. Volunteers, as in the Peace Corps, return to their past life and to freedom. It is unfortunate that members of religious orders prize themselves and their spiritual orientation so little.

When we work with and for the poor and disadvantaged, it is true that we may give better witness by identification with them in their physical environment. But unless we share our facilities and talents and resources, we have merely descended to their level without helping them to rise to a higher level. There seems to have been a time in history when sharing the life style of the poor was a very persuasive testimony to the following of Christ; this may have been predicated on the assumption that people could not move very easily anyway from one social or economic class to another. In modern times we see a great fluidity of wealth and of the levels of society. Therefore, the poor are not automatically impressed simply because we share their lot. They want to be shown how to rise to a higher standard of living. For example, a missionary in South America, while presenting himself as willing to live in the milieu of a back-country farmer, must assist his people to arrive at a higher standard of living by improved techniques and contacts with the twentieth century—whether it be a matter of credit unions or brick-making. The missionary to the poor, recognizing human value, exposes the poor to a better life. In the process he hopes that the poor will have more time for study, will achieve leisure, and will investigate the meaning of life through religion. In other words, where religious once taught implicitly through poverty that it was virtuous to share the lot of the suffering Christ when it was inescapable, now they are called upon to emphasize that it is not virtuous to be disadvantaged if it is possible to escape the situation. This is, once more, the service-aspect of their total ministry. The nineteenth-century Franciscan missions of California are a parade example. The apostolic life of poverty must be interpreted differently according to local needs of the apostolate. The general Constitutions of an institute must be broad enough to provide such flexibility.

In the progressive countries where advanced technology is a substantial factor in the way of life, religious are called upon to demonstrate that the modern life can be more than crassly materialistic. The humanistic psychologists point out the opposition between Technology and Eros—that is, between the inexorable machine and the liberating power of human love-relationships. An outstanding example of the real compatibility of the two in a context of poverty was the saintly Franciscan and martyr of charity, Maximilian M. Kolbe. He was optimistic, for he accomplished his life's work with less than one lung. He made himself accessible to the spiritual needs of his time by printing a daily newspaper and many periodicals in his native Poland. He was mobile enough to establish a similar, flourishing foundation in Japan. He was innovative in using airplanes to make deliveries and in planning to make popular movies and set up television broadcasts as early as 1939, when war broke out in Europe. He creatively allowed his *several hundred* friars at Niepokalanow to develop patents and to build the largest and most efficient printing plant in Central Europe. Yet the personal poverty of the friars there is still a legend.

In Chapter Two of the *First Rule* St. Francis seems to set

a general norm of his Order's poverty: "The brothers are free to receive anything that the poor are accustomed to have, with the exception of money." Chapter Fifteen forbids the brothers to ride horseback or to have a beast of burden, because poor folk generally did not. It would have been incongruous for a brother to arrive on horseback in the morning and ask a farmer to work in his fields for payment in produce or ask a weaver for a bolt of cloth at the end of the day. Candidates had to dispossess themselves; if that was impossible because of prior commitments, their good will sufficed. In the *First Rule*, unlike the *Second*, the Founder permitted money for the care of the sick friars and lepers (Chapter Eight). St. Francis probably had no other apostolates that required ready cash at the time he wrote the *First Rule*; there were neither houses of formation nor seminaries for clerical candidates. But the principle is nevertheless established by this provision and another directive of the *First Rule* which was applicable to lay-brother candidates and then extended to priest members; that is, they were to possess the tools necessary to the trade they practiced upon entering—utensils, instruments, pots, or whatever. Since the Gospel points out that Christ had a treasurer among the Twelve, St. Francis' attitude is at first difficult to grasp. Perhaps he saw that money was the chief symbol of the competitive and materialistic middle class just beginning to emerge in the thirteenth century. He himself knew how it had enabled him to lead a life of selfish indulgence as a youth. He likewise saw that the financial security and storehouses of the existing monasteries kept the monks from living in contact with other men and earning their keep along with and by means of preaching God's word and serving others.

St. Francis said he would gladly strip the altar of the Virgin Mary to give to those really in need; her Son would send someone to restore to his mother what she had lent to the poor. Yet he did not look down upon and judge the rich; they were to help support good persons who were living the ascetical life of service. In nothing were the brothers to judge others, especially the wealthy (*Second Rule*, Chapter Two). Above all, if they did have to beg, they were to demonstrate the spirit of joy in privation. St. Francis seemed to have a particular block about money as such, but he did not hesitate to receive all of Monte Alverno as an outright gift from Count Orlando Chiusi. Once more, personal experiences conditioned a Founder to incorporate certain points into the Rule. It almost seems a fixation with St. Francis: "If we should happen to find money anywhere, let us not consider it more than dirt under our feet...Should any brother collect or possess money or coin [except for the necessities of the sick, as was mentioned], all the rest should consider him a false brother, a thief, and a robber—the owner of a purse—unless he were really to have a change of heart" (*First Rule*, Chapter Eight.) Nevertheless the general attitude of the saint on poverty is insightful and is magnificently recorded by his biographer: "To the degree that the brothers neglect poverty, the world will neglect them. They will seek, but not find. But if they lean on our Lady Poverty, the world will support them, precisely because they have been given to the world for its salvation" (Celano, *Second Life*).

CHAPTER XII

Law and Obedience

I noted in the prior chapter that the vows presuppose each other and help make them operative. Obedience is certainly a species of poverty, because it eminently requires emptying out oneself and dispossession of self. At times everyone feels "trapped" in one's career, vocation, marriage, job, school, friendships, and other relationships. In his own First Order St. Francis took note of this entrapment, because one has to love the community which seemed even disloyal and traitorous. A religious who prefers to suffer persecution rather than be separated from his confreres, certainly perseveres in true poverty and obedience, because he lays down his life for his brethren (John 15:13). No matter where they are, the friars must always remember that they have given themselves up completely and handed over their entire selves to our Lord Jesus Christ, and so they should be prepared to expose themselves to every enemy, visible or invisible, for the love of him.

Cajetan Esser, O.F.M., in his important study, *Origins of the Franciscan Order*, points out how unique our Founder was. Because so many of Francis' innovations have become ordinary in religious and spiritual life, the particularly Franciscan dimension may be lost. Each community was like a center to which the itinerant friars would return, while they did not observe a cloister in the monastic sense of sequestration. They returned to base to pray, reflect, and share, as one would expect from a closely-knit family. From time to time they left for solitary places to pray and rest in the Lord, as did Francis and Christ before him.

Superiors were bound to the common life. Until Francis' time, Benedictine abbots typically lived apart from the larger community of monks. They had special quarters, sometimes a separate building, even a private kitchen and other marks of privilege. The local abbots were the living rule and authority for the whole monastery. They decreed the forms of liturgy, work projects, and in general controlled the life styles of everyone. St. Francis, on the other hand, required centralization around the common rule and habit. The freedom he endorsed for his friars related to personal life style. Friars did not vow "stability of place," whereby they had to remain their whole lives in a particular jurisdiction or community. St. Francis merely warned his followers "not to wander outside obedience," the *locale of their assignment* and general supervision of the guardian or perhaps the custos. They worked in fields, barns and warehouses with manual labor and lowly tasks and never made managerial decisions.

To reinforce the chapter decisions and the government centered around the Rule, the ministers were to visitate the friaries regularly, spend time sharing the community's life, and correct any lapses in religious discipline. The ministers were to correct sinners and give them a penance, unless, not being priests themselves, the ministers had to send them to a priest for absolution. In fact, those who could not live the Rule spiritually were mandated to have recourse to the ministers. It appears that an abbot's regulations were not questionable, but the Franciscan local superior and even the Rule could be questioned by the friar.

Chapters were an important part of Franciscan life. They were a time of instruction and sharing the experiences from all parts of the Order. During chapters assignments were made and plans to expand the Order were formalized. Later, however, chapters led to a democratic movement by 1230 (after Francis died) as they became the law-making and judicial agency for the friars.

The amazing fact was that the Church approved these novelties and departures from existing religious Orders. No doubt we can lay up their success to the absolute Franciscan obedience to the Roman See and the non-threatening attitude of the Founder, unlike other innovators of the day, who criticized the Church and society.

If one were to apply these innovations to the present, they would entail the following notions: Although we are not bound to one location or ministry in "stability," we are not to seek a bailiwick or assignment that separates us from the community. One could be greatly successful in an individual apostolate, yet fail as Franciscans if he or she were divorced from a frequent, daily exchange with one's own co-religious. This is the ideal of fraternal obedience which requires poverty of self. To go aside and find quiet time and space has always been a value, to find a new and different environment to foster prayer—retreats, days of recollection, study days. The superior who does not share the assignments of others may be failing as a role model—a personal car or easy chair in the recreation room, privileges for his friends and relatives, first choice in all matters. Such marks may emphasize authority, but diminish the sense of service. Individuals have different capacities and limitations. The amount of time off, spending money, choice of assignment differ, but equality in the Order means the same opportunities for spiritual and intellectual growth, and equal opportunity to be heard out and respected.

Without reading the "signs of the times," the Church, which includes all its members, would stagnate. It may be legitimate for other sectors of the Church to criticize the policies and non-doctrinal statements of the official Church. But the attitude of St. Francis is proper to all who bear the title of Franciscan: the most profound reverence for the Holy Father and the bishops in communion with him (even if for some personal reason one has some misgivings). In a wider sense, outsiders should have a welcome into Franciscan places and find it without divisiveness and the discomfort of criticism. The Franciscans do not have to agree with others' critiques, but they ought to show charity and be non-judgmental themselves, and perhaps gently influential.

The theological framework of Franciscan obedience is Pauline in reference, although inspired by the Gospel. St. Paul appears somewhat legalistic: the Old Law is set aside by the merits of Jesus, who conquers sin, death, and the law itself. This is the point of the Letter to the Romans, but in Galatians Paul underscores that the only thing that counts is becoming a new creation. The Gospel presses a new identity upon us, because nature is too little, too weak by itself.

As someone once wrote in a charming metaphor, when mankind got "off the track" with original sin, Jesus did not simply use his cross as a derrick, as it were, to put the train back on the rails. Instead he built a whole new railroad, the new creation. To paraphrase the Franciscan Duns Scotus, Jesus would have become incarnate (and railroad designer) regardless of whether we had stayed on track or not, in order to provide the way to the Father. No one knows the track to the Father unless the Son reveals it. As the new creation we have the potential to become divine by sharing God's own love life and ultimately rising to a spiritualized personhood in resurrection.

The Church is the sign of how God wants men and women to live: as a city set on a hill, a light on the lampstand, leaven in the mass of dough, and as salt of the earth. Francis deeply immersed himself into the mysticism of the Church and made his Order a "city set on a hill," visibly making religious life the common property of all believers. Francis showed that the Gospel life was possible to anyone anywhere anytime. The Franciscan, primarily a follower of Jesus, asks not only what Jesus said and did, but what he would do in our place right now. Otherwise we remain derailed, unreformed children of Adam and Eve, still the old creation, still placing ourselves under the law, not yet "Church."

Everyone is a unique variable, bonded to Jesus in a special way, a composite of personal experiences drawn from his or her education, ethnicity, parentage, friendships, religious background, and so forth. This uniqueness or composite focuses in those strengths we call our charism, a replication of some aspect of the life of Christ. Thus we need Jesus not only to find the Father; we need Jesus to find out who we are. Because no one is born outside the realm of God's grace, we cannot become complete persons without somehow bonding with Jesus.

As St. Paul wrote, we have to complete in our persons what was lacking in the redemption of the world by Christ. The ultimate meaning of the gospel will not be discovered until the return of Jesus. In the Acts of the Apostles we read how the Jewish-Christian community changed into worldwide Christianity by obedience to the Pentecostal Spirit. Franciscans became part of the many crusades for justice and peace, for protecting life from the womb to old age, for political and educational ethics. All this is part of Franciscan obedience to God's mandate to serve and preserve, to be "stewards of the mysteries of God" (I Cor. 4:1). They give thanks on behalf of those who fail to thank God or who were unaware that they are beneficiaries of grace. This is another kind of obedience to the natural sentiments of gratitude God placed in us.

We can summarize Francis' vision of obedience to the Church. For him detailed structure was unnecessary, but he respected and cherished the institution that keeps the Word and Sacrament among us. Nevertheless the Church *effectively* assembles wherever Jesus is made present in that community by the living out of Gospel values and when the members are obedient to the Spirit. Obedience to the Holy Spirit is always the theological foundation of holiness. The obedience of religious must stem from that theological foundation. The twelfth century was a stable society regardless of the rise of communes and guilds. Everyone's role was predictable. Doctrine had largely been spelled out; every situation was foreseen by moralists. Childhood baptism required no "conversion." The hierarchy organized Church activities and orderliness made religion routine. Holiness was the end product of rituals and sacraments to an almost "magical" degree. Thus the time of St. Francis was not an age of risk-taking. As in our time the preservation of the Catholic faith was paramount, and everyone's role was clearly defined. There was little attack on the *status quo.* "Boat-rockers" were not welcome on the ship of Peter.

St. Francis, however, was a "boat-rocker." All he addressed, however, was the complacency of the churchmen. Yet he was merely obedient to the Gospel. Every believer accepts this. But St. Francis provided a new kind of "religious" person, who brought heart and humanity to formal religion. St. Francis was not afraid of becoming a person on the fringe of society, without clout and status. The great difference between Francis and the others of his day is that Francis did not use his authority to empower and revolutionize the poor. He simply pointed out that power did not make people happy, and that Christ was also deprived of his rights.

The role opposites of those who obey are those in authority. A careful meditation on the life of Christ as we read the gospels is that although Christ possessed all authority and "all power in heaven and on earth was committed to him," he never seems to have exercised power and authority over others, but only over the demons or evil spirits of possession. What Jesus exercised over others was *influence,* rather than power and authority. He wanted the strength of his teaching to change lives. We note also in St. Francis' relationships with his brothers, sisters, and laity, that he avoided force or mandates of obedience. He preferred example, exhortation, and persuasion that led to ongoing conversion. This last refers to one's true meaning, what arises from your relationship, rather than from your function as teacher, nurse, counselor, administrator, etc.

One's relevance to the Church and world should not derive from what a layperson can do as well as you, but from your *sacramentality*—a visible sign productive of grace, the Christian's essential mission. (We can only be the instrument of grace, not its cause, which is only God himself!) The problem is not our being in the world, but the world being in us. Besides being sacramental, Franciscans, in defining their obedience to the Spirit, are expected to be counter-cultural and a sign of contradiction. If we don't make time for people, we are too busy. If we associate only with those of our own apostolate, we are too preoccupied. If we exclude from our company those who are of a different age, theological position, devotional life, or interests, then we are not yet Christian, much less Franciscan. We have become too sophisticated to be simple.

The first result is that we give the impression that we do not need others. The second is that we cannot or fail to live tentatively and at risk, ready to be obedient to God's call. We shouldn't compromise our ideals of obedience, but be realistic about our ability to achieve them.

Surrender your immediate gratifications for the long-range goals of community. Don't demand your rights, defend your ego, feel sorry for yourself for days, nor carefully guard your words— so no one knows who you really are! Once more: risk self-disclosure, especially about your vision and ideals. (We don't talk enough about spiritual things; are we embarrassed?) We have been over-instructed about introspection, but not how to share ideas and feelings.

Once a friar was telling me that he had lost his vocation and was planning to leave our community. At the time I simply asked one question that turned him around: What ever happened to carrying the cross? He was stunned and answered, "I forgot all about that!" So in community you have to be resolved to suffer and follow God's time line and not your deadline.

Obedience is the most difficult vow to understand and practice in an age of democracy and personalism. This vow must also be seen in the light of the Franciscan charism, particularly its self-expression and mobility. Another factor in this charism, optimism about man's perfectibility and good will, should characterize superiors in their trust of the subject's convictions and insights.

The presence of a superior should bring one greater security that he is being loyal to and sharing in the mission of the Church, rather than inflating his ego. Praise and acknowledgment—those very important functions of a superior—serve to reinforce the subject's zeal and to buffer his frustrations. Some contemporary authors reject the word "subject" in religious life, for one is subject only to God. Rather, they say, one should refer to "co-workers." Whereas this has considerable merit in view of St. Paul's mention of his own "co-workers" in the Church, "subject" puts a religious in the mind of Christ—the supreme identification in the life of a Christian: Christ was subject to Mary and Joseph in all things, subject to Jewish rituals during his ministry in Palestine, and subject unto death under Roman law.

When we read of the Church in the Acts and the Epistles, we do not see authoritarianism, however. Peter himself served and in a sense obeyed the mandates of the believing community, particularly the voice of the Apostolic College. In Chapter Eight of the Acts, we read that it was they who sent Peter and John to lay hands on the Christians of Samaria in order that the latter might receive the Spirit. We do not read much about the assertions of authority in the Apostolic Age. The numbers of Christians were few enough to be like a family or fraternity. Since they commonly held that the return of Christ was imminent, there did not seem to be much purpose in a "staff and line" organization anyway. Meanwhile, whoever had most closely witnessed the significant acts and words of the Master automatically enjoyed the greatest influence. From this we can at least glean a concept that a superior arises to leadership from knowing the mind of Christ, rather than being adept in sensitivity sessions or knowledgeable in the apostolic techniques of the local community. One hopes, of course, that a superior knows both Christ and the skills of the twentieth century.

Psychologists state that an important task in the maturation process is an increasing tolerance of reasonable frustration. Setting aside the problem of those neurotics who become superiors at times (because they actively seek office or have it thrust upon them), some subjects are simply unable to tolerate reasonable frustration, perhaps because of childhood experiences or a lack of the spirit of the *anawim*. They should recognize themselves as unsuited to religious life, especially if they find themselves hostile to a superior who gives evidence of zeal and optimism himself. It is just that not everyone has received the gift to obey. We easily grant that not every superior has the ability to clarify his thinking to his subjects. St. Teresa of Avila once remarked that she would prefer a learned to a pious spiritual director (she was not speaking of a superior in this case), if she could not have both. Notwithstanding her preference, most subjects would be reassured if they knew that the superior habitually listened to God during prayer as his primary obligation to his subjects. We remember that the theological and canonical experts advised the Pope not to approve St. Francis' charism at the outset. Assuming now that God intended the work of the saint to flourish, we read that only one Cardinal came forward to support the movement; he said refusal would be tantamount to saying that the gospel is an impossible ideal.

Let us examine the words and actions of St. Francis himself and set them in the context of the life the first followers actually lived. At first glance it seems as if he legislated the kind of obedience that contemporary authors are disparaging. As we examine his words and acts, it is necessary to distinguish the statements of a perfected and heroic soul about his personal virtue from the actual legislation for the imperfect and typical person who enters religious life as a "school for perfection." St. Francis commands us by his legislation; he draws us by his example. Every person decides for himself what the basis for his obedience will finally be.

It was written of Francis that he made a corpse-like obedience his own option. He once said that he would even let wild beasts devour him without struggling, because their strength and ferocity were given to them by the Lord. To the extent that denial of one's instinct for self-preservation is irrational (since there is no motive here of dying for another), one cannot make it part of the Franciscan charism. To the degree that such statements symbolize subjection to the *known* will of God, no one would oppose them. We have to recognize and contend with many dramatic remarks of St. Francis. "Do not mention impossibilities. Were I to command anything beyond your natural strength, then obedience would become strong enough for it" (Celano, *First Life*). Though a superior who conducts himself according to this principle may note with satisfaction that the subject was, indeed, able to be pushed a little further, one would hope that he is also able to see whether he is pushing his subject closer to a mental and spiritual breakdown.

Elsewhere St. Francis asserts that he would obey a novice of an hour's standing as quickly as a wise and experienced brother, since "the less important the one who governs, the greater the subjection of the one governed" (Celano, *Second Life*). Although one is tempted to think that no one would presume to command the Founder during his lifetime, as a matter of fact, when the provincials demanded a written constitutional form of government rather than a day-to-day commentary by him, St. Francis dramatically resigned his patriarchal authority and promised obedience to Peter Cataneo, his vicar. He asked the latter to place a superior over him, moreover, so that he would continue to grow in grace. Further, acceding to the voices of the elected ministers and at the behest of his friend Cardinal Hugolino, he wrote the *First Rule* of twenty-three chapters—despite his lifelong discomfort with written documents and what he feared might be rationalizations about the Gospel life. Even so, despite his protestations of subjection, in the incontrovertible words of his later *Second Rule* of 1223 he still considered himself the supreme arbiter of the Franciscan Order: "The brothers are obliged to obey Brother Francis and his canonically elected successors" (Chapter One). It seems, therefore, that St. Francis never intended to alter his role as mentor of the Order, but was willing to live in subjection with respect to his daily conduct, for he says in his final *Testament*, "I wish to be a prisoner in the guardian's keep, so that I may not take a step or perform an action outside obedience and his desires, for he is my lord."

Apart from the personal life of the Founder, we can learn

much about the life style and obedience of the first friars. In the same document, the *Testament*, St. Francis writes, "All the brothers are obliged to obey their guardians." Apparently not all the friaries had such a superior, because further on he directs the brothers to report any lapses of faith or liturgy to the *nearest* guardians. In the *Second Rule* he also distinguishes between a *house* and a *place*. We must keep in mind the astounding liberty of the first decades of the First Order—greater than religious ever enjoyed before or after in any of the major foundations in the history of the Church. The brothers were almost entirely "laics" at first, not "clerics." Like the *braceros* of the United States, they went off for the day or for many days to earn some payment (in the friars' case, it was payment in kind, not in money). In this way the brothers supported themselves and the poor. Because they "free-lanced" continually, they were not bound to seek constant permissions, make many reports, or follow a conventual routine—until the priestly and monachizing element prevailed in the Order. This fluid life style was possible only when the friars were neither tied to cultic and sacramental ministrations as priests, nor bound to regulated institutional life as teachers or nurses. In any case, St. Francis would consider it incredibly complicated to expect subjects to wear a path to the superior's door as most existing Constitutions require. He gives general directives about obedience in the *First Rule*. The brothers should gladly serve and obey *each other* in the spirit of charity. (This is analogous with fraternal correction, which is not left to superiors alone.) The professed, he writes, should not wander about, beyond the pale of obedience. This seems to refer to the daily manual labor mentioned above.

In fact, the founder always seemed more preoccupied with the functions and personality of the superiors rather than with those of the subjects. In Chapter Four of the *First Rule*, Francis concerns himself with the role of the minister as being more crucial than that of a guardian. The ministers are to visit the brothers *often*, admonish and console them, and remember that the Savior came to serve, not to be served. They are to give good example, lest they have to answer for the loss of any brothers on judgment day. In Chapter Five of the same Rule, St. Francis uses the hendiadys "ministers and servants" seven times to reinforce the concept of service. Nowadays we read a great deal about *diakonia* as the primary dimension of authority in the Apostolic Age. The other diminsions are *marturi*, the witnessing to Christ's life by the testimony of his saving action in oneself, and *koinonia*, the fellowship of community action. These three components of authority in the early Church, when set alongside St. Francis' life and writings, reinforce the validity of the assertion that his charism was to restore the Apostolic Age to the Church. Perhaps nowhere does this attitude come through more clearly than in St. Francis' description of an ideal minister general in the *Second Life* by Celano. He is to be a man without inordinate attachments, fond of prayer, and responsive to individual needs without favoritism. He should project the image of simplicity rather than learning. He ought not to be fixated on hobbies or collections, lest this distract him from his office, which is a burden more than an honor. Fully available to others, he must console the afflicted, being their ultimate fraternal comfort. Otherwise, with no place left for them to go for healing, the disease of despair will undo them. In order to teach meekness to the high-spirited, he has to lower himself and not thrust his authority upon them. Finally, he must demonstrate the tenderest pity to the lost sheep who have deserted the Order, because the temptations that would drive a man to such desolation must be overwhelming, indeed.

As in the primitive Church, a lay Order, such as St. Francis originally had in mind, needed little display of jurisdiction. When pulpit-preaching and sacramental administration became extensive activities of the Order, St. Francis incorporated directives into the *Second Rule* about clerics' activities in relationship to bishops. Already when St. Francis wrote to St. Anthony in Sicily about teaching the brothers theology, the number of clerics in the Order was growing; here was the beginning of our seminaries of theology. At the Chapter convoked on May 23, 1260, when the Constitutions of Narbonne were being compiled from all the earlier decrees and interpretations since the time of the Founder, St.

Bonaventure forbade the admission of "lay brothers" into the Order, except when domestic chores required it—and then they were to be admitted only with the permission of the minister general. Other prescriptions were written into the general law that St. Francis may have wondered about. Despite his wanting even the walls to be rubbed with meat at Christmas, the eating of meat was never allowed inside the friary, a monastic practice. The young friars were ordered to confess twice weekly and receive Holy Communion at least fifteen times a year—which in those days would be considered very frequent reception. The friars also had to have a companion when they left the friary. Finally, the voluntary fast after Epiphany mentioned by St. Francis in the Rule was made mandatory thereafter.

We realize in retrospect that St. Bonaventure had to contend with separatist, even heretical elements in the Order. But whether all of his measures and inhibitions clarified or obscured the mind of the Founder must be judged likewise in retrospect. When the Cardinal Protector of the Poor Clares, Giovanni Gaetano Orsini, who was later to be elected Pope Nicholas III, asked St. Bonaventure to take back jurisdiction over the Second Order, the latter insisted that the Clares maintain a strict enclosure and that they have the support of endowments and funds without depending on their neighbors' largesse. Neither was according to the mind of St. Francis and St. Clare, who were very relaxed in their personal relationship. On her deathbed Clare was at pains to secure the Pope's written confirmation of her "privilege of poverty." The point of this digression in a chapter on obedience and laws is that, while the existential personality of an Order does imply evolution, the multiplication of laws by authority, especially if the body politic is not consulted, is likely to impede, rather that facilitate the expression of a charism. For this reason, during the post-Vatican-Council renewal of religious life, legislation is the last, not the first act of a General Chapter. Our understanding of the mechanics of government, such as length of term of office and the manner of election, is much less important than understanding the balance between *institutional* and *charismatic* elements of religious life. Wherever there is no clear command in canon law, on the one hand, or in a Founder's description of his charism, on the other, considerable discretionary powers should be left to the local superior—or, rather, the subject himself. This is merely an intelligent application of the principle of *subsidiarity* .

In order for law to be most effective in *freeing* people to serve God, those who live under it should have an extensive voice in its formulation, so that it is already an "internalized" conviction. Law is a coin with two faces. One side is changeless: the nature of man's psychological makeup, the authority of God over man, the example of Christ as the supreme "law of the Gospel," and especially the charism of the institute. A candidate to the Order or a member knows that these elements are not contestable. The reverse side of the coin has changeable elements, but the value remains the same, even though the mint mark and date give us added information about the time and place from which the coin came. Constitutions and interpretations are similar to the changing inscription of the coin. This side of the "coin of law" represents the expectations and self-understanding of the membership in differing ages and circumstances. These expectations become the Constitutions that keep the charism alive; they are not an inviolable "sacred cow." St. Francis himself had a problem with this; he did not at first want "glosses" on the Rule, which is the nature of Constitutions. He heard that some superiors were interpreting his Rule quite flexibly, and so he gave general permission to the *entire* Order to disobey whatever was not "to the letter." Cardinal Hugolino saved the day by countermanding St. Francis, who obeyed without question.

In this last matter St. Francis shows considerable ambivalence. In his final *Testament* he forbade glosses on the *Rule*, yet from about 1212, when annual Chapters became typical, he framed many statutes to interpret his charism. This was even prior to the General Chapters that began five or six years later. The whole process, according to the *Legend of the Three Companions*, consisted in collecting Gospel quotations with a brief exegesis. They say that he tried many rules before he wrote one down. Among the *Opuscula* edited by the Quaracchi Franciscans, there is a letter to a minister general, possibly Brother Elias, written by the Founder. St. Francis interprets some points of his Rule and asserts, "For these and whatever other points in the Rule that are not so clearly stated, you will with God's help provide fulfillment." When some personal or apostolic need arises, St. Francis gives his followers full freedom. "In a moment of obvious necessity the brothers should act as the Lord inspires, for necessity has no law" (*First Rule*, Chapter Nine).

The provincial or local superior should ask his subjects as a group to establish their self-expectations and their expectations of each other. Once this is clarified, his obligation is to see to it that these expectations are met. Thus any individual opposition represents alienation from the community, rather than a private conflict with the authority. Further, this enables the superior to become the focus of the community's apostolate and social life. He gives the means to an apostolic end, once he understands the subjects' purpose, without having to seek permission from higher superiors. The immediate superior merely asks to be informed of the subject's needs and progress for two reasons. If he is successful, the subject can be praised and reinforced. If unsuccessful, the subject can be buffered, his feelings protected, the pieces picked up for a fresh start—and the superior can take some of the blame emanating from higher authority, since we assume that he has greater interior resources and graces in his post.

The superior forbids and prohibits whatever imperils the personality and life style of the Order with one hand, and releases the spiritual energy of his subjects with the other. Personal freedom does not confer the liberty to *thwart* the law, since even on a local level the members have formulated the law, but it constrains one to *act out* the convictions by which he has freely bound himself. The difficulty is to locate and train superiors who would be of this mind. St. Francis realized this. In Chapter Eight of the *Second Rule* he provided for the deposition of a minister who was a poor servant of the brotherhood. And when a subject felt that he couldn't observe the Rule conscientiously under some local conditions, he was to have recourse to the minister, who is ordered to apply the "golden rule." In this passage St. Francis does not seem to believe in so-called "blind obedience." He remembers the attitude of Christ, who called his followers "friends," no longer "servants," because the Holy Spirit would soon descend to give an understandable rationale to "everything I have commanded you" [to observe]. In both his Rules St. Francis is careful to exempt a subject from a command contrary to conscience. The implication is that one might have to obey God against the superior. But one must be willing to take the consequences, even as Christ did before the Sanhedrin and Pilate. Whereas one is released from obedience to a superior, one is not free from paying the price, while maintaining interior and exterior peace for the good of the Order. A Franciscan who would rather remain in the Order within a situation of persecution and frustration, especially if he is sincerely trying to follow his conscience and be loyal to the charism of St. Francis, will be blessed by the saint in time and eternity.

The ultimate truth each religious experiences for himself is this: a person can be free every day of his life even if he decides every day of his life to be bound by another's will.

Fr. Anselm W. Romb OFM CONV.
Conventual Franciscan Friars
Marytown
1600 W. Park Ave.,
Libertyville IL 60048-2593
U. S. A.

Holy Thursday, 1995